P9-ASG-195

Scott Foresman

# Grammar and Writing Practice Book

**Editorial Offices:** Glenview, Illinois • Parsippany, New Jersey • New York, New York
**Sales Offices:** Boston, Massachusetts • Duluth, Georgia • Glenview, Illinois
Coppell, Texas • Sacramento, California • Mesa, Arizona

ISBN: 0-328-14626-9

**Copyright © Pearson Education, Inc.**

All Rights Reserved. Printed in the United States of America. This publication, or parts thereof, may be used with appropriate equipment to reproduce copies for classroom use only.

11 V004 14 13 12 11 10 09

## Unit 1 Meeting Challenges



## Unit 2 Doing the Right Thing



## Unit 3 Inventors and Artists

## Unit 4 Adapting



## Unit 5 Adventurers



## Unit 6 The Unexpected

## Grammar Extra Practice

## Standardized Test Preparation



## Unit Writing Lessons

# Grammar Lessons

Name ______________________

# Four Kinds of Sentences and Interjections

Each kind of sentence begins with a capital letter and has a special end mark.

A **declarative sentence** makes a statement. It ends with a period.
A teacher needs a sense of humor.

An **interrogative sentence** asks a question. It ends with a question mark.
Have you read this joke book?

An **imperative sentence** gives a command or makes a request. It ends with a period. The subject (*you*) does not appear, but it is understood.
Tell us a joke, please.

An **exclamatory sentence** shows strong feeling. It ends with an exclamation mark.
What a hilarious punch line that was!
I can't believe you said that!

An **interjection** is a word or a group of words that expresses strong feeling. It is not a complete sentence.
Ha, ha! What a funny joke!

**Directions** Rewrite each sentence. Make any needed corrections in capitalization and punctuation.

**1.** darius played jokes on people?

______________________

**2.** that rubber snake scared me to death.

______________________

**3.** would he play a joke on the teacher.

______________________

**Directions** Complete each sentence with words from the box. Then write whether the sentence is *declarative, interrogative, imperative,* or *exclamatory.*

| at the size of that book! | is an interesting subject. |
|---|---|
| the assignment for me. | need a class in reading? |

**4.** Language arts ______________________

**5.** Do we really ______________________

**6.** Wow, look ______________________

**7.** Copy down ______________________

**Home Activity** Your child learned about four kinds of sentences. Have your child write about an event at school using one example of each kind of sentence.

Name ________________________________



# Four Kinds of Sentences and Interjections

**Directions** Complete each sentence by adding your own words and the correct end punctuation. The label tells what kind of sentence each should be.

**1.** A big pile of homework ________ (declarative)

______________________________________________

______________________________________________

**2.** Did Mrs. Granger ________ (interrogative)

______________________________________________

______________________________________________

**3.** Wow! This test ________ (exclamatory)

______________________________________________

______________________________________________

**4.** This report ________ (declarative)

______________________________________________

______________________________________________

**5.** Please buy me ________ (imperative)

______________________________________________

______________________________________________

**Directions** What is the most unusual homework assignment you ever had? Write three sentences describing the assignment. Make each sentence a different kind.

______________________________________________

______________________________________________

______________________________________________

______________________________________________

**Home Activity** Your child learned how to use four kinds of sentences in writing. Have your child write about his or her homework routine, including at least one declarative, one interrogative, one imperative, and one exclamatory sentence.

Name ____________________



# Four Kinds of Sentences and Interjections

**Directions** Read the paragraph. Mark the letter that identifies what kind of sentence each is.

(1) Middle school is a challenge for many students. (2) Are you moving from classroom to classroom this school year? (3) What a zoo the hallways are between classes! (4) The lock on my locker never opens properly. (5) Please be on time for class. (6) All the teachers make this request. (7) How can I make it on time? (8) I can barely get my locker open in four minutes.

**1.** **A** Declarative
**B** Interrogative
**C** Imperative
**D** Exclamatory

**2.** **A** Declarative
**B** Interrogative
**C** Imperative
**D** Exclamatory

**3.** **A** Declarative
**B** Interrogative
**C** Imperative
**D** Exclamatory

**4.** **A** Declarative
**B** Interrogative
**C** Imperative
**D** Exclamatory

**5.** **A** Declarative
**B** Interrogative
**C** Imperative
**D** Exclamatory

**6.** **A** Declarative
**B** Interrogative
**C** Imperative
**D** Exclamatory

**7.** **A** Declarative
**B** Interrogative
**C** Imperative
**D** Exclamatory

**8.** **A** Declarative
**B** Interrogative
**C** Imperative
**D** Exclamatory

**Directions** Circle the letter of the sentence that has correct end punctuation.

**9.** **A** Mr. Smith teaches science?
**B** What is your favorite subject.
**C** Fifth graders take several classes!
**D** They also have music and gym class.

**10.** **A** Jim is good in language arts!
**B** He has a huge vocabulary?
**C** Didn't he win the spelling bee?
**D** Hurray, he won again.

**Home Activity** Your child prepared for taking tests on kinds of sentences. Have your child read part of a story to you and identify each sentence as declarative, interrogative, imperative, or exclamatory.

Name ______________________________



# Four Kinds of Sentences and Interjections

**Directions** Add the correct end punctuation to each sentence. Then on the line write whether the sentence is *declarative, interrogative, imperative,* or *exclamatory.*

1. Do you like chewing gum ______________
2. Lucy stuck a wad of gum in her mouth ______________
3. Please spit that out ______________
4. Oh, no! I swallowed it ______________
5. Gum leaves a sticky mess on shoes ______________

**Directions** Underline the mistakes in each sentence. Write the correct letter or punctuation mark above each underline.

6. once I got gum stuck in my hair?
7. what an awful mess that was
8. rub this ice cube on the gum!
9. mom had to cut it out with scissors?
10. how do you like my new haircut
11. i think it looks great?

**Directions** Add your own words to complete each sentence. Write the new sentences. Be sure you use end punctuation correctly.

12. The rules for every class ______

______________________________________________

13. The rule about gum ______

______________________________________________

14. Don't ______

______________________________________________

15. Do you think ______

______________________________________________

**Home Activity** Your child reviewed four kinds of sentences. For five minutes, write down what you say to each other. Have your child identify each kind of sentence.

Name ______________________________

# Simple and Complete Subjects and Predicates

Every sentence has a subject and a predicate. The words that tell whom or what the sentence is about are the **complete subject.** The most important word in the complete subject is the **simple subject.** It is usually a noun or a pronoun. Some simple subjects have more than one word, such as *Kansas City.*

Many families moved west in the 1840s. The simple subject is *families.*

The words that tell what the subject is or does are the **complete predicate.** The most important word in the complete predicate is the **simple predicate,** or the verb. Some simple predicates have more than one word, such as *is walking*.

The trip could take up to six months. The simple predicate is *could take.*

A **fragment** is a group of words that lacks a subject or a predicate.

Had to carry everything with them. This fragment lacks a subject.

A **run-on** is two or more complete sentences run together.

The settlers needed food they needed tools.

**Directions** Underline each simple subject once. Underline each simple predicate twice.

1. A tornado's shape is like a funnel.
2. The deadly funnel measures up to a mile wide.
3. They are unpredictable in their movements.
4. Settlers feared the awful twister.

**Directions** Write *F* after a fragment. Write *R* after a run-on. Then correct the sentence errors. Write a complete sentence or two complete sentences on the lines.

5. The wind inside a tornado ________

______________________________

______________________________

6. A tornado can be called a twister it is also sometimes called a cyclone. ________

______________________________

______________________________

**Home Activity** Your child learned about subjects and predicates. Talk about a storm you and your child have experienced. Have your child write several sentences about the storm and identify the complete and simple subjects and predicates in each sentence.

# Simple and Complete Subjects and Predicates

**Directions** Use each noun and verb pair as the simple subject and simple predicate. Add words to make a complete sentence. Underline the complete subject once and the complete predicate twice.

**1.** tall tales include

______________________

______________________

**2.** hero is

______________________

______________________

**3.** stories make

______________________

______________________

**4.** Pecos Bill lassoed

______________________

______________________

**5.** Paul Bunyan rode

______________________

______________________

**Directions** This paragraph contains fragments and a run-on. Rewrite the paragraph. Add words and punctuation to make sure every sentence has a subject and a predicate.

Davy Crockett was a real person he was also the hero of many tall tales. A good frontiersman and hunter. Killed a bear when he was only three. This "king of the wild frontier."

______________________

______________________

______________________

______________________

**Home Activity** Your child learned how to write sentences that have subjects and predicates. Name a familiar person. Have your child write three sentences about the person and underline the subject and circle the predicate in each sentence.

Name ______________________________

# Simple and Complete Subjects and Predicates

**Directions** Mark the letter of the sentence in which the simple subject and simple predicate are correctly underlined.

1. **A** Cowboys of Texas herded cattle to Kansas on the Abilene Trail.
   **B** Cowboys of Texas herded cattle to Kansas on the Abilene Trail.
   **C** Cowboys of Texas herded cattle to Kansas on the Abilene Trail.
   **D** Cowboys of Texas herded cattle to Kansas on the Abilene Trail.

2. **A** The great herds moved along slowly.
   **B** The great herds moved along slowly.
   **C** The great herds moved along slowly.
   **D** The great herds moved along slowly.

3. **A** These large animals must graze for hours each day.
   **B** These large animals must graze for hours each day.
   **C** These large animals must graze for hours each day.
   **D** These large animals must graze for hours each day.

4. **A** They needed a vast supply of water.
   **B** They needed a vast supply of water.
   **C** They needed a vast supply of water.
   **D** They needed a vast supply of water.

5. **A** Lean, tanned cowboys urged the cattle forward.
   **B** Lean, tanned cowboys urged the cattle forward.
   **C** Lean, tanned cowboys urged the cattle forward.
   **D** Lean, tanned cowboys urged the cattle forward.

**Directions** Mark the letter of the group of words that has a subject and a predicate.

6. **A** Crossed dangerously swift rivers.
   **B** In the dark of night under the light of the moon.
   **C** The cowboys also protected the cattle from predators.
   **D** Sleeping in shifts on the hard ground.

7. **A** A cowboy's horse.
   **B** For miles in the hot, dusty country.
   **C** They shared water and companionship.
   **D** Became a best friend and a well-loved co-worker.

8. **A** A well-made hat was a prized possession.
   **B** Also a sturdy saddle and bridle.
   **C** Tough leather chaps for the legs.
   **D** Protected the cowboy's face from heat and dust.

**Home Activity** Your child prepared for taking tests on subjects, predicates, fragments, and run-ons. Circle a paragraph in the newspaper. Have your child identify the subject and predicate of each sentence in the paragraph.

Name ______________________________

# Simple and Complete Subjects and Predicates

**Directions** Draw a line between the complete subject and the complete predicate in each sentence. Circle the simple subject and the simple predicate.

1. A blacksmith was important to the pioneer community.
2. People called this metal worker a smithy.
3. He could mend a plow or tools.
4. The powerful man pounded steel on his anvil.
5. Fascinated children watched the smithy at work.

**Directions** Identify the part of the sentence that is underlined. Write *complete subject, simple subject, complete predicate,* or *simple predicate.*

6. Patient oxen <u>were once beasts of burden</u>. ______________________
7. <u>A pair of oxen</u> might pull a wagon. ______________________
8. These big animals <u>could plow</u> all day. ______________________
9. The <u>farmer</u> walked along behind. ______________________

**Directions:** Write *F* if a group of words is a fragment. Write *R* if it is a run-on sentence. Rewrite each one to make a complete sentence or a compound sentence.

10. Barbed wire was invented in Illinois it quickly became popular all over the United States. ______

______________________________________________________________

______________________________________________________________

11. Fenced in their cattle. ______

______________________________________________________________

______________________________________________________________

12. These fences kept cattle in and rustlers out cattle injured themselves on the fences at first. ______

______________________________________________________________

______________________________________________________________

**Home Activity** Your child reviewed subjects, predicates, fragments, and run-ons. Ask your child to make a note card for each term with the definition on one side and an example on the other.

Name ______________________

# Independent and Dependent Clauses

A related group of words with a subject and a predicate is called a **clause.** A clause that makes sense by itself is an **independent clause.** A clause that does not make sense by itself is a **dependent clause.** A **complex sentence** contains an independent and a dependent clause.

| | |
|---|---|
| **Independent Clause** | They came to the island in canoes. |
| **Dependent Clause** | even though it was a long trip |

If the dependent clause comes first, set it off with a comma: *Until they were attacked, Native Americans lived on the island.* If the independent clause is first, no comma is needed: *Native Americans lived on the island until they were attacked.*

**Directions** Write *I* if the underlined group of words is an independent clause. Write *D* if it is a dependent clause.

1. If you live on an island, you become independent. ________
2. Natives made their own clothes because they could not buy them. ________
3. Since there were no stores, they hunted for food. ________
4. A seal provided meat while people used its hide for clothes. ________
5. A hunting party paddled boats out to sea so that they could catch fish. ________
6. Women gathered berries and roots before winter came. ________
7. Because they needed containers for the food, they made baskets out of grasses. ________

**Directions** Underline the dependent clause in each sentence.

8. Because they cooked with fire, the natives kept live coals.
9. After food was prepared, they covered the embers with ashes.
10. While they slept through the night, the coals stayed warm.
11. The coals smoldered until morning came.
12. When the cook blew on the coals, they glowed brightly.
13. She fed wood to the coals so that the fire would catch again.
14. If her husband had caught fish that morning, they would eat well for breakfast.

**Home Activity** Your child learned about independent and dependent clauses. Ask your child to write a sentence about Native Americans using an independent clause and a dependent clause and explain the difference between the two.

Name ______________________

# Independent and Dependent Clauses

**Directions** Add an independent clause to each dependent clause to create a sentence that makes sense. Write the sentence.

1. because the natives depended on the sea for food

2. so that they could make a boat

3. after the tree was cut down

4. when the ashes were scraped out

5. since the boat was made by digging out wood

6. so that they would be watertight

7. because the boats were so well made

**Home Activity** Your child learned how to write sentences that combine an independent and a dependent clause. With your child, read an article about Native Americans. Have your child look for sentences that have both kinds of clauses.

Name ______________________

# Independent and Dependent Clauses

**Directions** Mark the letter of the sentence that contains both an independent clause and a dependent clause.

**1. A** Natives used different kinds of natural materials as tools.
**B** A sharp-edged rock could serve as a knife.
**C** Hot rocks were placed into the fire.
**D** When they got hot, they acted like an oven.

**2. A** Bones of some animals became tools too.
**B** Because bone is so hard, it can pass through leather.
**C** A long, thin piece of bone with a sharp end served as a needle.
**D** A large bone could serve as a club or even a ladle.

**3. A** Bones were also used as decoration.
**B** Artists might carve bone if the weather was bad.
**C** A knife of stone could slice into the bone.
**D** Some were cut into interesting shapes.

**4. A** Hides of animals provided clothing.
**B** The hide was scraped long and hard.
**C** Deerskin made soft, warm clothing after it was tanned.
**D** Tougher parts of the deerskin were suitable for moccasins.

**5. A** Natives on the seacoast gathered beautiful shells.
**B** Some colors and types of shells were especially valuable.
**C** These shells were used as a form of money for trade.
**D** Until white people arrived, gold and silver coins were unknown.

**6. A** The natives respected all forms of life.
**B** They depended on animals for food and clothing.
**C** They used every part of the animal so that nothing was wasted.
**D** Animals always appeared in Native American tales and myths.

**7. A** The coyote was respected because it was intelligent.
**B** It could be a competitor for small game and berries.
**C** Coyotes and humans are omnivores.
**D** They eat both animals and plants.

**8. A** The bison was the mainstay of life on the Great Plains.
**B** These huge beasts covered the plains until the late 1800s.
**C** White hunters killed bison for sport or for their tongues.
**D** Although most of the bison were killed, the species survived.

**Home Activity** Your child prepared for taking tests on independent and dependent clauses. Say a dependent clause (*after we eat dinner, before we leave home, when we go to the store*). Have your child add an independent clause to make a sentence.

Name ______________________________

# Independent and Dependent Clauses

**Directions** Write *I* after each independent clause. Write *D* after each dependent clause.

1. some Native Americans built homes of wood ________
2. where they lived year-round ________
3. others made tipis of skins and poles ________
4. so that they could move their homes ________
5. the cone-shaped tipi was useful ________
6. because it was efficient and portable ________
7. when the herd moved on ________
8. the tipis were quickly taken down ________
9. the natives followed the bison ________
10. until the herd reached new grazing land ________

**Directions:** Write sentences combining each pair of clauses in the first exercise. Use correct capitalization and punctuation.

11. (Clauses 1 and 2) ______________________________

______________________________

12. (Clauses 3 and 4) ______________________________

______________________________

13. (Clauses 5 and 6) ______________________________

______________________________

14. (Clauses 7 and 8) ______________________________

______________________________

15. (Clauses 9 and 10) ______________________________

______________________________

**Home Activity** Your child reviewed independent clauses and dependent clauses. With your child, look through a newspaper article. Have your child find sentences with independent and dependent clauses and mark the clauses *I* and *D*.

Name ________________________________

# Compound and Complex Sentences

A **simple sentence** expresses a complete thought. It has a subject and a predicate.
The Negro League formed in 1920.

A **compound sentence** contains two simple sentences joined by a comma and a conjunction such as *and, but,* or *or.*
The athletes played several games a day, and they traveled on a bus.

A **complex sentence** contains an independent clause, which can stand alone, and a dependent clause, which cannot stand alone. The clauses are joined by a word such as *if, when, because, until, before, after,* or *since.* In the following sentence, the independent clause is underlined once; the dependent clause is underlined twice.
Many years would pass before the major leagues were integrated.

**Directions** Join each pair of simple sentences with *and, but,* or *or.* Write the compound sentence on the lines. Change punctuation and capital letters as necessary.

**1.** My sister can hit the ball hard. She pitches well too.

________________________________

________________________________

**2.** The game should have started at one o'clock. A thunderstorm began at 12:45.

________________________________

________________________________

**3.** The teams will make up the game next Sunday. They will wait until the end of the season.

________________________________

________________________________

**Directions** Write *compound* after each compound sentence. Write *complex* after each complex sentence. Underline the word that joins the two clauses in each sentence.

**4.** All players are important to a team, but the pitcher may be most important. ____________

**5.** If a pitcher strikes out batters, the opposing team cannot score. ____________

**6.** Outfielders must catch the ball when the batter hits a pop fly. ____________

**7.** The game was tied, and no one left the bleachers. ____________

**8.** The pitcher struck out two batters, but the third batter hit a home run. ____________

School-Home CONNECTION

**Home Activity** Your child learned about compound and complex sentences. Have your child write a paragraph about a baseball game, using at least one compound sentence and one complex sentence.

Name ______________________________

# Compound and Complex Sentences

**Directions** Add a clause from the box to complete each sentence. Write *compound* or *complex* to tell what kind of sentence each one is.

| |
|---|
| He was the first African American player in the white major leagues |
| and a hero's skin color does not matter to them |
| the jeers soon turned to cheers |
| Since Jackie Robinson was the only African American on the field |
| and in 1962 he was elected to the Baseball Hall of Fame |

**1.** Baseball fans love the stars of the game, ______________________________
______________________________. ______________

**2.** ______________________________
______________________________, he endured anger and jeers at first. ______________

**3.** Because he showed great skill and grace, ______________________________
______________________________. ______________

**4.** The public admired Robinson, ______________________________
______________________________. ______________

**5.** ______________________________
______________________________, but he soon was not the only one. ______________

**Directions** Write several sentences about your favorite sports hero or performer. Use at least one compound sentence and one complex sentence. Use commas and conjunctions correctly.

______________________________
______________________________
______________________________
______________________________
______________________________
______________________________

**Home Activity** Your child learned how to use compound and complex sentences in writing. Ask your child to read you a story and to point out examples of compound and complex sentences.

Name ______________________________



# Compound and Complex Sentences

**Directions** Mark the letter of the phrase that correctly identifies each underlined word, group of words, or sentence.

**1.** Every day Ted and I play catch, or we join our friends in a game.
**A** dependent clause
**B** independent clause
**C** compound sentence
**D** complex sentence

**2.** We love the game, but we aren't the best players.
**A** conjunction
**B** independent clause
**C** dependent clause
**D** complex sentence

**3.** If you practice every day, you will do better.
**A** dependent clause
**B** independent clause
**C** compound sentence
**D** complex sentence

**4.** A game is more fun when the crowd cheers you on.
**A** dependent clause
**B** independent clause
**C** compound sentence
**D** complex sentence

**5.** Although our team played well, we still lost.
**A** dependent clause
**B** independent clause
**C** compound sentence
**D** complex sentence

**6.** Rub this oil into your glove, and you will catch balls more easily.
**A** dependent clause
**B** independent clause
**C** compound sentence
**D** complex sentence

**7.** Before you play a big game, you should relax.
**A** conjunction
**B** dependent clause
**C** independent clause
**D** complex sentence

**8.** Aleesha plays third base, or she is catcher.
**A** conjunction
**B** independent clause
**C** compound sentence
**D** complex sentence

**9.** We keep score, but we really play just for fun.
**A** dependent clause
**B** independent clause
**C** compound sentence
**D** complex sentence

**10.** Because we have fun, we don't mind an occasional loss.
**A** dependent clause
**B** independent clause
**C** compound sentence
**D** complex sentence

**Home Activity** Your child prepared for taking tests on compound and complex sentences. Have your child read a sports article in the newspaper and identify compound sentences and complex sentences.

Name ______________________

# Compound and Complex Sentences

**Directions** Join each pair of simple sentences to form a compound sentence. Use the conjunction that makes sense (*and, but,* or *or*). Put a comma before the conjunction. Write the compound sentence on the lines.

**1.** Julia loves sports.
She cannot decide which one to try first.

______________________

______________________

**2.** She could play softball.
She could join a soccer team.

______________________

______________________

**3.** Her older brother plays on a traveling soccer team.
Her mom is an umpire for the softball league.

______________________

______________________

**4.** Marcus runs like the wind.
He is quite strong.

______________________

______________________

**Directions** Write *compound* after each compound sentence and underline the conjunction. Write *complex* after each complex sentence and underline the dependent clause.

**5.** His name was George Herman Ruth, but everyone called him Babe. ______________

**6.** He was a left-handed pitcher when he began his career in 1914. ______________

**7.** He pitched 163 games, and he won 92 of them. ______________

**8.** If you can believe it, he was greatest of all at hitting home runs. ______________

**Home Activity** Your child reviewed compound and complex sentences. Ask your child to explain how a game is played, using some compound and complex sentences.

Name ______________________



# Common and Proper Nouns

The names of particular persons, places, and things are **proper nouns.** Capitalize the first word and each important word of a proper noun.

I love Harry Potter in the books by J. K. Rowling.

All other nouns are **common nouns**. They are not capitalized.

That author has written five best-selling novels.

Capitalize the first word and all important words in a title.

*Reflections on a Gift of Watermelon Pickle*

Capitalize days of the week and months of the year.

Saturday, October 14

Capitalize the first letter of an abbreviated proper noun. Abbreviations often occur in addresses, titles and initials in names, and names of days and months. Most abbreviations end with a period. In addresses, state names are abbreviated using two capital letters and no period.

The envelope went to Mr. L. Cho, 11 E. 3rd St., Rochester, MN 55901.
It was postmarked Mon., Nov. 6.

**Directions** Write the proper noun from the box that matches each common noun. Add capital letters where they are needed.

| | |
|---|---|
| sears tower | *my side of the mountain* |
| argentina | president jefferson |
| rebecca | "america the beautiful" |

| Common Noun | Proper Noun |
|---|---|
| **1.** girl | ______________ |
| **2.** president | ______________ |
| **3.** country | ______________ |
| **4.** book | ______________ |
| **5.** building | ______________ |
| **6.** song | ______________ |

**Home Activity** Your child learned about common and proper nouns. Take a walk with your child. Have him or her pick out proper nouns on signs and buildings in your community and practice writing them using proper capitalization.

Name ______________________________

# Common and Proper Nouns

**Directions** Rewrite each sentence. Capitalize all proper nouns.

**1.** Many immigrants to the united states came to new york.

______________________________

______________________________

**2.** The statue of liberty and the empire state building inspired them.

______________________________

______________________________

**3.** Men like john d. rockefeller and jacob astor had become rich in america.

______________________________

______________________________

**4.** Even a poor person could one day live at 1600 pennsylvania ave., washington, d.c.

______________________________

______________________________

**Directions** Add the date, greeting, signature, and information needed in the body of the letter. Use correct capitalization.

______________________

Dear ____________________,

Please come to a birthday party for ____________________ (person) on ____________ (day of week), ____________________ (date), at ________ (time of day). The party will be held at

____________________________ (name of place)

____________________________ (address)

____________________________

We really hope you can come and help us celebrate.

Best wishes,

____________________________ (signature)

**Home Activity** Your child learned how to use common and proper nouns in writing. Ask your child to write a note inviting a friend to a special event. He or she should capitalize all proper nouns.

Name ______________________________

# Common and Proper Nouns

**Directions** Mark the letter of the correct answer.

1. **A** mr. william baird, jr.
   **B** Mr. William Baird, jr.
   **C** Mr. William Baird, Jr.
   **D** mr. William Baird, jr.

2. **A** sunday, march 14
   **B** Sunday, March 14
   **C** Sunday, march 14
   **D** sunday, March 14

3. **A** Sugarland, TX 77478
   **B** Sugarland, tx 77478
   **C** sugarland, TX 77478
   **D** Sugarland, Tx. 77478

4. **A** dr. wilson adair
   **B** dr. Wilson adair
   **C** Dr. wilson Adair
   **D** Dr. Wilson Adair

5. **A** Rome, italy
   **B** rome, italy
   **C** Rome, Italy
   **D** rome, Italy

6. **A** a park on the Missouri River
   **B** a Park on the Missouri river
   **C** a park on the missouri River
   **D** a Park on the missouri river

7. **A** the movie *Beauty and The Beast*
   **B** the movie *beauty and the beast*
   **C** the Movie *Beauty And the Beast*
   **D** the movie *Beauty and the Beast*

8. **A** 190 n. Clark st.
   **B** 190 N. Clark St.
   **C** 190 n. Clark St.
   **D** 190 N. Clark st.

9. **A** *a Light in the Attic*
   **B** *A Light in The Attic*
   **C** *A Light In The Attic*
   **D** *A Light in the Attic*

10. **A** Miss Anna kowalski
    **B** miss Anna kowalski
    **C** Miss Anna Kowalski
    **D** miss Anna Kowalski

**Directions** Match each capitalization rule with the mistake in each sentence. Write the letter on the line.

**A** Capitalize the first and all important words in a book title.
**B** Capitalize days of the week and months of the year.
**C** Capitalize the first letter of an abbreviated proper noun.
**D** Capitalize titles before people's names.

_____ **11.** Did you know major Segal was born in Romania?

_____ **12.** He wrote a book called *coming to america*.

_____ **13.** The group meets the first monday in each month.

_____ **14.** April's meeting is at the library on w. Oak st.

**Home Activity** Your child prepared for taking tests on common and proper nouns. Have your child read an interesting magazine or newspaper article. He or she can circle the proper nouns and underline the common nouns.

Name ______________________

# Common and Proper Nouns

**Directions** Match the letter of each common noun on the right with a proper noun on the left. Then write another proper noun that fits in that category.

____ **1.** Japan ______________________ **A.** city

____ **2.** *Oliver Twist* ______________________ **B.** country

____ **3.** Ms. Kopeki ______________________ **C.** team

____ **4.** Atlanta Braves ______________________ **D.** book

____ **5.** London ______________________ **E.** teacher

**Directions** Write *C* if the group of words is capitalized correctly. If the group of words is not capitalized correctly, rewrite it using correct capitalization.

**6.** Helen and her cousins ______________________

**7.** mr. Jorge Ruiz, sr. ______________________

**8.** the greatest City in the Midwest ______________________

**9.** fourth of july ______________________

**10.** Mississippi River ______________________

**11.** holidays in november ______________________

**12.** south bend, In 46614 ______________________

**Directions** Rewrite each sentence. Use capital letters where they are needed.

**13.** On friday we went to a restaurant on east 18th st. called hot tamales.

______________________

______________________

**14.** It is owned by ms. marie dablontez, who is from mexico.

______________________

______________________

**Home Activity** Your child reviewed common and proper nouns. Ask your child to write a note inviting a friend to do something. Have him or her check to be sure proper nouns are capitalized correctly.

Name ______________________



# Regular and Irregular Plural Nouns

**Plural nouns** name more than one person, place, or thing.

- Add *-s* to form the plural of most nouns.
  swing/swings    animal/animals
- Add *-es* to nouns ending in *ch, sh, x, z, s,* and *ss*.
  fox/foxes    bush/bushes    church/churches
- If a noun ends in a vowel and *y*, add *-s*.
  monkey/monkeys    toy/toys
- If a noun ends in a consonant and *y*, change *y* to *i* and add *-es*.
  blueberry/blueberries    pony/ponies    penny/pennies
- Some nouns have **irregular plural** forms. They change spelling.
  woman/women    tooth/teeth    ox/oxen
- For most nouns that end in *f* or *fe*, change *f* to *v* and add *-es*.
  wife/wives    wolf/wolves    thief/thieves
- Some nouns have the same singular and plural forms.
  salmon    trout    sheep

**Directions** Underline the plural nouns in each sentence.

1. Caterpillars eat leaves constantly.
2. This one looks beautiful with its bright yellow stripes.
3. Those leaves come from maples, cherries, and oaks.
4. It looks as though it has many feet.
5. Bristles stick up on its back like little brooms.

**Directions** Cross out each incorrectly spelled plural noun. Write the correct spelling above the word you crossed out.

6. Nature makes many intricate patternes in bright colors.
7. From the oceans to the skys, we find swirles, zig-zags, circles, and archs of color.
8. In autumn leafs turn vivid colors and stand like brushs full of paint against the sky.

**Home Activity** Your child learned about regular and irregular plural nouns. Take a walk and have your child identify people, places, animals, and things in groups. Ask him or her to spell these plural nouns correctly.

Name ____________________

# Regular and Irregular Plural Nouns

**Directions** Write a sentence using the plural form of each noun.

**1.** woman

____________________

**2.** foot

____________________

**3.** monkey

____________________

**4.** deer

____________________

**5.** leaf

____________________

**Directions** Write the paragraph on the lines. Write the plural form of each noun in ( ). Add a word of your own to describe each plural noun. Write your own ending sentence for the paragraph.

Our scout troop collected ___ (coat) and (glove) for ___ (child). We made ___ (poster) and knocked on ___ (door). Many people gave ___ (donation). Sometimes ___ (family) searched their ___ (closet) to help us. We took ___ (bunch) of winter wear to the Salvation Army.

____________________

____________________

____________________

____________________

____________________

____________________

____________________

____________________

____________________

____________________

**Home Activity** Your child learned how to use plural nouns in writing. Have your child point out plural nouns on packages and labels and explain the rule for forming each plural.

Name ______________________________

# Regular and Irregular Plural Nouns

**Directions** Mark the letter of the word that correctly completes each sentence.

**1.** Dad found caterpillars eating his beloved rose ____.
**A** bushes
**B** bush's
**C** bushes
**D** bushies

**2.** Put two caterpillars in a jar with some ____.
**A** leafs
**B** leaves
**C** leafes
**D** leavs

**3.** I punched many ____ in the lid of the jar.
**A** holes
**B** hols
**C** hole
**D** holez

**4.** The caterpillars were soft as ____.
**A** bunnys
**B** bunnyes
**C** bunnies
**D** bunny

**5.** I had to gather ____ of grass and leafy twigs.
**A** bunches
**B** bunchies
**C** bunchen
**D** bunchs

**6.** One morning I was sure ____ had stolen them.
**A** thief
**B** thiefs
**C** thiefes
**D** thieves

**7.** Then I saw cottony ____ attached to twigs.
**A** capsules
**B** capsulies
**C** capsuls
**D** capsulen

**8.** They had sewn their ____ into cushions called pupas.
**A** body
**B** bodys
**C** bodeys
**D** bodies

**9.** Soon they would be winged ____.
**A** creature
**B** creatures
**C** creaturees
**D** creaturies

**10.** Their wings would have brilliant ____ of color.
**A** patchs
**B** patchies
**C** patches
**D** patch

**Home Activity** Your child prepared for taking tests on regular and irregular plural nouns. Have your child make flash cards with singular and plural forms of nouns on opposite sides. Use the cards to help him or her learn plural forms.

Name ______________________

# Regular and Irregular Plural Nouns

**Directions** Write the plural forms of the underlined singular nouns.

**1.** Are you good at drawing picture or painting scene?

______________________

**2.** Latoya loves art and has taken many art class.

______________________

**3.** An artist must consider the line, space, color, and texture of a painting.

______________________

**4.** A portrait artist paints pictures of lady and gentleman.

______________________

**Directions** Cross out each incorrectly spelled plural noun. Write the correct spelling above the word you crossed out.

**5.** These kindes of paintingz are called still life.

**6.** I will draw a picture of this bowl of peachs, peares, and bananas.

**7.** Unfortunately, they only look like circeles, ovals, and crescenties.

**8.** Janelle draws horse, sheeps, and piges well.

**Directions** Write each sentence. Write the plural forms of the nouns in ( ). Add your own describing word for each plural noun.

**9.** Some artists make ____ (craft) such as ____ (quilt) and ____ (pot).

______________________

______________________

**10.** ____ (dish) and ____ (tablecloth) can be ____ (work) of art.

______________________

______________________

**Home Activity** Your child reviewed regular and irregular plural nouns. Ask your child to list things you have in your kitchen and write the plural form for each noun.

Name ______________________________

# Possessive Nouns

A **possessive noun** shows ownership. A **singular possessive noun** shows that one person, place, or thing has or owns something. A **plural possessive noun** shows that more than one person, place, or thing has or owns something.

- To make a singular noun show possession, add an apostrophe (') and *-s*.
  a bird's song
- To make a plural noun that ends in *-s* show possession, add an apostrophe (').
  several weeks' work
- To make a plural noun that does not end in *-s* show possession, add an apostrophe (') and *-s*.
  the women's papers

**Directions** Write each noun as a possessive noun. Write *S* if the possessive noun is singular. Write *P* if the possessive noun is plural.

1. friends ________________ ______
2. story ________________ ______
3. freedom ________________ ______
4. mornings ________________ ______
5. children ________________ ______
6. milk ________________ ______

**Directions** Add an apostrophe (') or an apostrophe (') and *-s* to make each underlined word possessive. Write the sentence on the line.

7. A diplomat life requires travel.

______________________________________________

8. Would democracy followers win the struggle?

______________________________________________

**Home Activity** Your child learned about possessive nouns. Have your child look at some sale ads and make up sentences about them using possessive nouns.

Name ______________________________

# Possessive Nouns

**Directions** Make each sentence less wordy by replacing the underlined words with a possessive noun phrase. Write the sentence on the line.

1. The pride of a son in his father can inspire him all his life.

______________________________

2. The rights of fathers are strong in Japanese society.

______________________________

3. The wishes of a father should always be respected by his family.

______________________________

4. The status of an elderly relative is highest of all.

______________________________

5. What is more, the commands of government officials must be obeyed by all.

______________________________

______________________________

6. The wants of an individual are less important than the well-being of the nation.

______________________________

______________________________

**Directions** Write a paragraph describing some of the traits of people in your family. Use possessive nouns to make your writing smooth and less wordy.

______________________________

______________________________

______________________________

______________________________

______________________________

______________________________

______________________________

**Home Activity** Your child learned how to use possessive nouns in writing. Have your child make labels for the belongings of different family members using possessive nouns.

Name ______________________



# Possessive Nouns

**Directions** Mark the letter of the word that correctly completes each sentence.

**1.** ____ Jews fled from the German soldiers.
**A** Polands
**B** Poland's
**C** Polands'
**D** Polands's

**2.** American ____ efforts helped win the war.
**A** soldiers
**B** soldier's
**C** soldiers'
**D** soldiers's

**3.** A ____ shoes wore out quickly.
**A** soldiers
**B** soldier's
**C** soldiers'
**D** soldiers's

**4.** Success often depended on the ____ food supply.
**A** armies
**B** armie's
**C** armys'
**D** army's

**5.** Soldiers carried several ____ cold rations.
**A** days
**B** day's
**C** days'
**D** days's

**6.** Many ____ stomachs were often empty.
**A** refugees
**B** refugee's
**C** refugees'
**D** refugees's

**7.** A ____ kindness kept them alive another day.
**A** strangers
**B** stranger's
**C** strangers'
**D** strangers's

**8.** Money might be sewn into ____ coat linings.
**A** women's
**B** woman's
**C** womens'
**D** womans'

**9.** Worry haunted the refugee ____ eyes.
**A** childrens
**B** children's
**C** childrens'
**D** childrens's

**10.** ____ stories seemed unbelievable.
**A** Survivors
**B** Survivor's
**C** Survivors'
**D** Survivors's

**Home Activity** Your child prepared for taking tests on possessive nouns. Have your child write several sentences describing a favorite toy or game using possessive nouns (such as *the bear's nose* or *the pieces' shapes*).

Name ______________________________

# Possessive Nouns

**Directions** Write each sentence. Change the underlined phrase to show possession.

**1.** The honesty of children is refreshing.

______________________________

**2.** The comment of one little boy was especially moving.

______________________________

**3.** The eyes of the grown-ups were red from lack of sleep.

______________________________

**4.** Did they sleep on the benches of the park?

______________________________

**Directions:** Cross out each incorrect possessive noun. Write the correct possessive form above the word you crossed out.

**5.** Some children held their fathers hands.

**6.** One little girls' coat was too small for her.

**7.** The little girl looked warm and happy in Sukios' coat.

**8.** Small acts of kindness made the outcast's lives better.

**Directions** Write a paragraph describing a refugee family that the Sugiharas might have helped. Use possessive nouns correctly.

______________________________

______________________________

______________________________

______________________________

______________________________

______________________________

**Home Activity** Your child reviewed possessive nouns. Ask your child to write sentences telling what he or she appreciates about home, family, school, and friends. Ask your child to try to use a possessive noun in each sentence.

Name ______________________

# Action and Linking Verbs

A complete sentence has a subject and a predicate. The main word in the predicate is a **verb**. An **action verb** tells what the subject does.

The little boy *cried* often.

A **linking verb** links, or joins, the subject to a word or words in the predicate. It tells what the subject is or is like.

He *seemed* very quiet. He *was* a good sport.

- Action verbs show actions that are physical (*hike, build*) or mental (*remember, approve*).
- Common linking verbs are forms of the verb *be* (*am, is, are, was, were*).
- These verbs can be linking verbs: *become, seem, appear, feel, taste, smell,* and *look.* (*The cake appears fresh. It looks tasty.*) However, some of them can also be used as action verbs. (*A boy appeared suddenly. He looked at the food.*)

**Directions** Write the verb in each sentence of the paragraph. Then write *A* if the verb is an action verb. Write *L* if it is a linking verb.

**1.** Are you a spoiled child? **2.** A spoiled child always gets his or her way. **3.** He or she seems selfish. **4.** Parents pamper the child too much. **5.** This treatment often leads to misery. **6.** The world responds better to a kind, unselfish person. **7.** Compassion is good for the giver and the receiver. **8.** The most unselfish people appear happiest.

**1.** ______________ ______ **5.** ______________ ______

**2.** ______________ ______ **6.** ______________ ______

**3.** ______________ ______ **7.** ______________ ______

**4.** ______________ ______ **8.** ______________ ______

**Directions** Write a verb from the box to complete each sentence. On the line after the sentence, write *A* if the verb is an action verb. Write *L* if it is a linking verb.

| combine | is | showed | are |
|---|---|---|---|

**9.** The dragon ______________ popular in Chinese culture. ______

**10.** In ancient China, people ______________ great respect for dragons. ______

**11.** Dragons ______________ not real animals. ______

**12.** They ______________ traits of many animals. ______

**Home Activity** Your child learned about action and linking verbs. Read a story together. Have your child point out several action verbs and linking verbs.

Name ______________________________

# Action and Linking Verbs

| celebrate | drink | ring |
|---|---|---|
| write | sways | dress |

**Directions** Use an action verb from the box to complete each sentence. Write the sentence.

1. People from around the world ________ the new year.
______________________________________________
2. In China, some people ________ as dragons.
______________________________________________
3. The dragon's tail ________ as it parades down the street.
______________________________________________
4. Children in Belgium ________ letters to parents on decorated paper.
______________________________________________
5. In the United States, people ________ a toast to the new year.
______________________________________________
6. Bells ________ out at midnight.
______________________________________________

**Directions** Write a paragraph describing a celebration. Use vivid action verbs and appropriate linking verbs. Underline the verbs you use.

______________________________________________
______________________________________________
______________________________________________
______________________________________________
______________________________________________
______________________________________________
______________________________________________

**Home Activity** Your child learned how to use action and linking verbs in writing. Ask your child to write a description of dinnertime at your home using action verbs and linking verbs.

Name ______________________________

# Action and Linking Verbs

**Directions** Mark the letter of the phrase that correctly identifies the underlined word in the sentence.

1. In ancient China, the Three Letters custom was important to a marriage.
   **A** action verb (physical)
   **B** action verb (mental)
   **C** linking verb
   **D** not a verb

2. The Betrothal Letter formally announced the engagement.
   **A** action verb (physical)
   **B** action verb (mental)
   **C** linking verb
   **D** not a verb

3. After that, a Gift Letter was necessary.
   **A** action verb (physical)
   **B** action verb (mental)
   **C** linking verb
   **D** not a verb

4. The letter listed gifts for the wedding.
   **A** action verb (physical)
   **B** action verb (mental)
   **C** linking verb
   **D** not a verb

5. She approved the proposed marriage.
   **A** action verb (physical)
   **B** action verb (mental)
   **C** linking verb
   **D** not a verb

6. The Wedding Letter was the third formal document.
   **A** action verb (physical)
   **B** action verb (mental)
   **C** linking verb
   **D** not a verb

7. The groom's family presented this letter to the bride's family.
   **A** action verb (physical)
   **B** action verb (mental)
   **C** linking verb
   **D** not a verb

8. It formally accepted the bride into the groom's family.
   **A** action verb (physical)
   **B** action verb (mental)
   **C** linking verb
   **D** not a verb

9. The bride usually brought a dowry of jewels and furniture.
   **A** action verb (physical)
   **B** action verb (mental)
   **C** linking verb
   **D** not a verb

10. Today, these wedding customs seem unusual.
    **A** action verb (physical)
    **B** action verb (mental)
    **C** linking verb
    **D** not a verb

**Home Activity** Your child prepared for taking tests on action and linking verbs. With your child, read a newspaper article. Have your child circle action verbs and underline linking verbs in the article.

Name ______________________

# Action and Linking Verbs

**Directions** Underline the verb in each sentence. Write *A* on the line if the verb is an action verb. Write *L* if it is a linking verb.

**1.** A governess raises a child in a private home. ________

**2.** She is important to the family. ________

**3.** She teaches the child his or her lessons. ________

**4.** However, a governess is much more than a teacher. ________

**5.** She shares playtime and mealtime with children. ________

**6.** She soon seems like one of the family. ________

**Directions** Match the verb with the phrase that correctly identifies the verb. Write the letter of the phrase on the line.

________ **7.** marries

________ **8.** becomes

________ **9.** wonders

________ **10.** happy

**A.** linking verb

**B.** action verb (physical)

**C.** not a verb

**D.** action verb (mental)

**Directions** Rewrite each sentence. Add your own verb to make the sentence clear and interesting.

**11.** People ________ candles and incense for different reasons.

______________________________________________

**12.** Candlelight ________ a soft, mysterious mood.

______________________________________________

**13.** Fragrant incense ________ pleasant.

______________________________________________

**14.** The pleasing light and scent ________ into the air.

______________________________________________

**15.** In this way, people ________ holy beings.

______________________________________________

**Home Activity** Your child reviewed action and linking verbs. Ask your child to write a letter to a friend or family member using some vivid action verbs and some linking verbs.

Name ______________________________

# Main and Helping Verbs

Verbs that are made up of more than one word are **verb phrases.** In a verb phrase, the **main verb** names the action. The **helping verb** helps tell the time of the action. Some common helping verbs are *has, have, had, am, is, are, was, were, do, does, did, can, could, will, would,* and *should.*

- The main verb is always the last word in a verb phrase. (A bird *is looking* at me.)
- There may be more than one helping verb in a verb phrase. (She *has been studying* animals a long time.)
- Helping verbs such as *is* and *are* show that action is happening in the present. (Annamae *is reading* about ecosystems.) *Was* and *were* tell that the action happened in the past. (The class *was reading* about animals last month.) *Will* tells that the action is going to happen in the future. (We *will study* extinct animals next week.)

**Directions** Underline the verb phrase in each sentence. Put one line under each helping verb and two lines under the main verb.

**1.** I have watched animals for years.

**2.** Right now I am watching birds at the feeder.

**3.** Some birds will visit the feeder dozens of times.

**4.** The chickadees have eaten all the thistle seeds.

**5.** A bright red cardinal is singing cheerfully.

**6.** Within two days, the birds will have emptied the feeder.

**7.** I can tell that moment.

**8.** The birds will be sitting on bushes by my window.

**9.** They are reminding me of their hunger.

**10.** Bird watchers should fill the feeder often.

**Home Activity** Your child learned about main and helping verbs. Have your child model an activity such as making a sandwich. Ask him or her to explain the job using sentences with verb phrases.

Name ____________________



# Main and Helping Verbs

**Directions** Underline the verbs and verb phrases in each paragraph. Circle the verb phrase that expresses the wrong time. Write the correct verb phrase on the line.

**1.** We are eating more fruits and vegetables these days. For example, for lunch I am having a veggie burger. It smells great. Cheese was melting on the top of it now.

____________________

**2.** Last week we drove to a state park. Dad had been studying forest plants. He had brought along his plant identification book. Soon we all are looking for ferns. Bobbie yelled. He had fallen in a stream!

____________________

**3.** This winter our family will visit a coral reef. Shelly may test her scuba gear. I will snorkel in the clear ocean water. We did marvel at the colorful fish and coral formations.

____________________

**4.** I am teaching the dog a trick. She loves her treats. She is getting a treat for her trick. She sits at the mere sight of the box. Was she learning? What do you think?

____________________

**Directions** Write a paragraph about an animal you have watched. Use some verb phrases.

____________________

____________________

____________________

____________________

____________________

____________________

____________________

____________________

**Home Activity** Your child learned how to express time correctly using verb phrases. Ask your child to use *be* verbs with action verbs to make up sentences about something he or she did in the past, is doing now, and will do in the future.

Name ______________________________

# Main and Helping Verbs

**Directions** Mark the letter of the words that correctly identify the underlined word or words in the sentence.

**1.** People should drive less.
**A** helping verb
**B** main verb
**C** verb phrase
**D** not a verb

**2.** Exhaust fumes are polluting the environment.
**A** helping verb
**B** main verb
**C** verb phrase
**D** not a verb

**3.** Certain chemicals will kill fish.
**A** helping verb
**B** main verb
**C** verb phrase
**D** not a verb

**4.** Runoff from farms may contain these chemicals.
**A** helping verb
**B** main verb
**C** verb phrase
**D** not a verb

**5.** Oil tankers have spilled millions of gallons of oil.
**A** helping verb
**B** main verb
**C** verb phrase
**D** not a verb

**6.** Fish, birds, and mammals are coated with the oil.
**A** helping verb
**B** main verb
**C** verb phrase
**D** not a verb

**7.** Without help they soon will die.
**A** helping verb
**B** main verb
**C** verb phrase
**D** not a verb

**8.** Many towns are putting garbage in landfills.
**A** helping verb
**B** main verb
**C** verb phrase
**D** not a verb

**9.** Plastics do not break down easily.
**A** helping verb
**B** main verb
**C** verb phrase
**D** not a verb

**10.** We are poisoning ourselves slowly.
**A** helping verb
**B** main verb
**C** verb phrase
**D** not a verb

**Home Activity** Your child prepared for taking tests on main and helping verbs and verb phrases. Have your child write sentences about his or her day's activities using verb phrases and point out main and helping verbs.

Name ______________________________

# Main and Helping Verbs

**Directions** Choose a helping verb from the box to complete each sentence. Write the sentence on the line. Underline the verb phrase.

| could | should | has | was | had | did |
|---|---|---|---|---|---|

1. Jane Goodall ________ studied African animals for decades.

______________________________

2. She ________ raised in England.

______________________________

3. Even as a little girl, she ________ always loved animals.

______________________________

4. In the jungle, Jane ________ watch chimpanzees for hours.

______________________________

5. She ________ not notice the hours passing.

______________________________

6. We ________ admire such devotion to animals.

______________________________

**Directions** Find the verb phrases. Underline each helping verb. Circle each main verb.

7. A wildlife refuge may provide the only safe habitat for some animals.
8. Many animals have been hunted too much.
9. Scientists have predicted the extinction of some species.
10. Animals in trouble are described as endangered.
11. Many groups are working to protect endangered animals.
12. Without our help, these animals will disappear like the dodo.

**Home Activity** Your child reviewed main and helping verbs. Ask your child to make up sentences using verb phrases to describe an animal's past, present, and future actions.

Name ______________________

# Subject-Verb Agreement

The subject and verb in a sentence must **agree,** or work together. A singular subject needs a singular verb. A plural subject needs a plural verb.

Use the following rules for verbs that tell about the present time.

- If the subject is a singular noun or *he, she,* or *it,* add *-s* or *-es* to most verbs.
  The wagon *creaks*. It *lurches* along.
- If the subject is a plural noun or *I, you, we,* or *they,* do not add *-s* or *-es* to the verb.
  The oxen *pull* the wagon. They *strain* uphill.
- For the verb *be,* use *am* and *is* to agree with singular subjects and *are* to agree with plural subjects.
  I *am* hot. Thomas *is* happy. The patriots *are* loyal. We *are* late.
- **A collective noun** names a group, such as *family, team,* and *class*. A collective noun is singular if it refers to a group acting as one: The family *is taking* a vacation. A collective noun is plural if it refers to members of the group acting individually: The family *are arguing* about the destination.

**Directions** Match each subject with a verb that agrees. Write the letter of the correct verb on the line.

| | | |
|---|---|---|
| ________ | **1.** The colonists | **A.** are training. |
| ________ | **2.** The British king | **B.** is beginning. |
| ________ | **3.** A war | **C.** rebel. |
| ________ | **4.** Troops | **D.** sends his army. |

**Directions** Underline the verb in ( ) that agrees with the subject of each sentence.

**5.** The American colonies (trade, trades) with England.

**6.** Two of the colonies' exports (is, are) cotton and indigo.

**7.** England (tax, taxes) the items imported into the colonies.

**8.** Tea (is, are) a popular drink in the colonies.

**9.** The Boston Tea Party (show, shows) the colonists' anger about taxes.

**10.** Today, Americans (drink, drinks) more coffee than tea.

**11.** Earlier conflicts (is, are) forgotten.

**12.** The two countries (consider, considers) themselves close allies.

**Home Activity** Your child learned about subject-verb agreement. Have your child make up sentences about clothes he or she wears, using both singular subjects (shirt, belt) and plural subjects (socks, shoes) and making sure verbs agree.

Name ______________________________

# Subject-Verb Agreement

**Directions** Add a verb to complete each sentence. Be sure to use the correct verb form.

**1.** The Liberty Bell __________________ a well-known American symbol.

**2.** It __________________ in the Liberty Bell Center in Philadelphia.

**3.** Many tourists __________________ this site.

**4.** __________________ the bell ever ring?

**5.** No. A crack __________________ up the side of the bell.

**6.** The main metals in the bell __________________ copper and tin.

**7.** The bell __________________ 2,080 pounds.

**8.** Philadelphia __________________ in southeastern Pennsylvania.

**9.** More than a million and a half people __________________ there.

**10.** Tourists __________________ the many historic sites in Philadelphia.

**Directions** Circle the verb that agrees with each subject. Then write sentences using at least three of the subject-verb pairs.

| | | |
|---|---|---|
| **11.** class | is studying | are studying |
| **12.** historic site | inspire | inspires |
| **13.** teacher | tell | tells |
| **14.** some students | sing | sings |
| **15.** they | is | are |
| **16.** I | feel | feels |

______________________________________________________________

______________________________________________________________

______________________________________________________________

______________________________________________________________

______________________________________________________________

**Home Activity** Your child learned how to write subjects and verbs that agree. Ask your child to make up sentences in the present tense describing favorite animals, first using a singular subject, then a plural subject (dog/dogs, lion/lions, and so on).

Name ______________________________

# Subject-Verb Agreement

**Directions** Mark the letter of the verb that agrees with the subject in the sentence.

**1.** Many poems ____.
**A** rhyme
**B** rhymes
**C** rhimes
**D** rhiming

**2.** I ____ the poems of Longfellow.
**A** enjoy
**B** enjoys
**C** enjoies
**D** enjoying

**3.** His work ____ both rhyme and rhythm.
**A** use
**B** uses
**C** using
**D** user

**4.** "The Midnight Ride of Paul Revere" ____ a narrative poem.
**A** be called
**B** are called
**C** is called
**D** be

**5.** Narrative poems ____ a story.
**A** telling
**B** tells
**C** tell
**D** telled

**6.** Poetry ____ vivid word pictures.
**A** paint
**B** painting
**C** painter
**D** paints

**7.** Our class ____ in unison.
**A** recite
**B** reciting
**C** recites
**D** recities

**8.** We ____ to do choral readings.
**A** like
**B** likes
**C** liking
**D** be liking

**9.** It ____ like a song.
**A** be
**B** being
**C** are
**D** is

**10.** The rhyming words ____ good to me.
**A** sound
**B** sounding
**C** sounds
**D** soundies

**Home Activity** Your child prepared for taking tests on subject-verb agreement. Have your child copy some subject and verb pairs from a favorite book and explain why the subjects and verbs agree.

Name ______________________________

# Subject-Verb Agreement

**Directions** Underline the subject of each sentence. Circle the verb in ( ) that agrees with the subject.

1. Paul Revere (is, are) a legendary figure of the Revolutionary War.
2. Americans (love, loves) hearing about his midnight ride.
3. I (imagine, imagines) that night.
4. Three men (ride, rides) from Boston to Concord.
5. Danger (lurk, lurks) around every bend.
6. An English scout (yell, yells) "Stop! Who goes there?"
7. His companions (stop, stops) one of the three riders.
8. One man (go, goes) no further that night.
9. It (is, are) Paul Revere.
10. Few people (know, knows) that fact.

**Directions** Add a present tense verb to complete each sentence. Be sure the verb agrees with the subject in number.

11. This portrait ____________________ a serious man.
12. It ____________________ a portrait of Paul Revere.
13. Several objects ____________________ on the table next to him.
14. They ____________________ a silversmith's tools.
15. The man's right hand ____________________ his chin thoughtfully.
16. His left hand ____________________ a silver teapot.
17. Americans still ____________________ the silver work of Revere.
18. A silver piece by Paul Revere ____________________ great value today.

**Home Activity** Your child reviewed subject-verb agreement. Ask your child to read a newspaper or magazine article and point out singular and plural subjects. Have him or her explain why the verbs agree with those subjects.

Name ______________________

# Past, Present, and Future Tenses

The **tense** of a verb shows when something happens. Verbs in the **present tense** show action that happens now. Some present tense singular verbs end with *-s* or *-es*. Most present tense plural verbs do not end with *-s* or *-es*.

An inventor creates a new tool. Inventions serve us well.

Verbs in the **past tense** show action that has already happened. Most verbs in the past tense end in *-ed.*

Not long ago, electronics changed the world.

Verbs in the **future tense** show action that will happen. Add *will* (or *shall*) to most verbs to show the future tense.

Many more inventions will appear.

- Some regular verbs change spelling when *-ed* is added. For verbs ending in *e*, drop the *e* and add *-ed*: *used, celebrated*. For verbs ending in a consonant and *y*, change the *y* to *i* and add *-ed*: *spied, lied*.
- For most one-syllable verbs that end in one vowel followed by one consonant, double the consonant and add *-ed*: *wrapped, patted.*
- Irregular verbs change spelling to form the past tense: *are/were, bring/brought, eat/ate, find/found, fly/flew, go/went, have/had, is/was, make/made, see/saw, sit/sat, take/took, tell/told, think/thought, write/wrote*.

**Directions** Write the correct present, past, and future tense of each verb.

| Verb | Present | Past | Future |
|---|---|---|---|
| **1.** jump | She ____________. | She ____________. | She ____________. |
| **2.** sit | He ____________. | He ____________. | He ____________. |
| **3.** worry | We ____________. | We ____________. | We ____________. |
| **4.** stop | It ____________. | It ____________. | It ____________. |

**Directions** Rewrite each sentence. Change the underlined verb to the tense in ( ).

**5.** Paul daydream about flying. (present)

______________________________________________

**6.** He study wingless flight. (past)

______________________________________________

**Home Activity** Your child learned about present, past, and future tenses. Have your child read a page in a story aloud, changing past tense verbs to present tense ones or present tense verbs to past tense ones.

Name ______________________________

# Past, Present, and Future Tenses

**Directions** Underline the verb or verbs that use the wrong tense. Write the correct tense.

**1.** Last year our class entered a reading contest. Stacks of books are everywhere. We visit the library often. A thousand books later, we won. ______________________

**2.** We will write book reports next week. I report on *Stuart Little*. It will be fun to read my report to the class. ______________________

**3.** *Babe* is a movie about an extraordinary pig. Babe gets along with all the animals on the farm. Babe helped the sheep and sheep dogs overcome their prejudice. ______________________

**Directions** Replace each underlined verb with the verb in the correct tense. Use the correct tense to make the order of events clear. Write the paragraph.

**4.** The era of winged flight for humans begin in 1903. **5.** That December Wilbur and Orville Wright fly their airplane at Kitty Hawk. **6.** Today, the world rely on air travel. **7.** Airplanes bring countries close. **8.** In the future, spacecraft carry you and me into space.

______________________________________________

______________________________________________

______________________________________________

______________________________________________

______________________________________________

**Directions** Pretend that you are Wilbur or Orville Wright. Write a paragraph about what you did to prepare for the first flight, what happened, and what you plan for the future.

______________________________________________

______________________________________________

______________________________________________

______________________________________________

______________________________________________

______________________________________________

______________________________________________

**Home Activity** Your child learned how to use present, past, and future tenses in writing. With your child, talk about an activity he or she completed, an ongoing activity, and a future activity.

Name ______________________________

# Past, Present, and Future Tenses

**Directions** Mark the letter of the verb that correctly completes the sentence.

**1.** Next week our class ____ a play.
**A** stage
**B** stages
**C** staged
**D** will stage

**2.** Two students ____ the play last summer.
**A** write
**B** writes
**C** wrote
**D** will write

**3.** Now we ____ in the classroom.
**A** rehearse
**B** rehearses
**C** rehearsed
**D** will rehearse

**4.** Our teacher ____ the director.
**A** is
**B** are
**C** were
**D** am

**5.** Last month I ____ for the lead.
**A** try out
**B** tries out
**C** tried out
**D** will try out

**6.** My parents always ____ I am a ham.
**A** say
**B** says
**C** saying
**D** will say

**7.** I was thrilled when I ____ the part.
**A** get
**B** gets
**C** got
**D** will get

**8.** I hope I ____ well on opening night.
**A** does
**B** done
**C** did
**D** will do

**9.** I am sure I ____ nervous.
**A** am
**B** are
**C** was
**D** will be

**10.** For now, Mom ____ me rehearse my lines every night.
**A** help
**B** helps
**C** helped
**D** will helping

**Home Activity** Your child prepared for taking tests on present, past, and future tenses. Have your child explain the present, past, and future tenses of verbs and give examples of each.

Name ________________________________

# Past, Present, and Future Tenses

**Directions** Identify the tense of each underlined verb. Write *past, present,* or *future.*

**1.** A play differs from a story in several ways. ______________

**2.** Stories have narrative and description. ______________

**3.** Plays consist almost entirely of dialogue. ______________

**4.** Shakespeare wrote some wonderful plays. ______________

**5.** Who were other great playwrights? ______________

**6.** One day I will act on the stage. ______________

**7.** Meanwhile, my dad encourages me. ______________

**8.** He tells me I have great stage presence. ______________

**9.** Once I took a drama class. ______________

**10.** We performed *A Charlie Brown Christmas.* ______________

**Directions** Rewrite each sentence twice. First, change the underlined verb to past tense. Then change it to future tense.

**11.** Hot air balloons are a unique way to fly.

Past: ________________________________

Future: ________________________________

**12.** We go on a ride in a hot air balloon.

Past: ________________________________

Future: ________________________________

**13.** The houses and cars below us look like toys.

Past: ________________________________

Future: ________________________________

**Home Activity** Your child reviewed past, present, and future tenses. With your child, list verbs that describe what your family does each day. Challenge your child to write the present, past, and future tenses of the verbs and use them in sentences.

Name ______________________



# Principal Parts of Regular Verbs

A verb's tenses are made from four basic forms. These basic forms are called the verb's **principal parts.**

| Present | Present Participle | Past | Past Participle |
|---|---|---|---|
| watch | (am, is, are) watching | watched | (has, have, had) watched |
| study | (am, is, are) studying | studied | (has, have, had) studied |

A **regular verb** forms its past and past participle by adding *-ed* or *-d* to the present form.

- The present and the past forms can be used by themselves as verbs.
- The present participle and the past participle are always used with a helping verb.

**Directions** Write the form of the underlined verb indicated in ( ).

1. For centuries, people admire the works of Leonardo da Vinci. (past participle)
______________________
2. Today he enjoy the title of greatest genius of the Renaissance. (present participle)
______________________
3. He observe everyday activities as a scientist. (past) ______________________
4. Leonardo paint with greater skill than any other artist of his time. (past)
______________________
5. He fill notebooks with his observations, illustrations, and original ideas. (past)
______________________
6. Scientists create working models from his instructions and drawings. (past participle)
______________________
7. Leonardo's life inspire me to be more observant. (past participle) ______________________

**Directions** Underline the verb in each sentence. Write *present, present participle, past,* or *past participle* to identify the principal part used to form the verb.

8. Leonardo lived in Vinci, Italy, as a boy. ______________________
9. Soon he had developed a keen eye and an observant nature. ______________________
10. Most people recognize the name Leonardo da Vinci 500 years after his death.
______________________

**Home Activity** Your child learned about principal parts of regular verbs. Ask your child to write the principal parts of *love, live,* and *dream* and then use each part in a sentence about himself or herself.

Name ______________________

# Principal Parts of Regular Verbs

**Directions** Write a complete sentence using the past participle form of the verb in ( ) with *have* or *has.*

**1.** Ms. Wissing (instruct) this art class for two years.

______________________

**2.** The students (enjoy) her hands-on teaching style.

______________________

**3.** For several weeks, our art class (study) how to draw life forms.

______________________

**4.** Tonya (sketch) the head of a woman.

______________________

**5.** I (complete) my drawing of a horse.

______________________

**6.** The teacher (encourage) my efforts in the past.

______________________

**Directions** Write a paragraph about something you have planned to invent or create. Include past participle forms of verbs where needed.

______________________

______________________

______________________

______________________

______________________

______________________

______________________

______________________

______________________

**Home Activity** Your child learned how to write principal parts of regular verbs correctly. Ask your child to write about a project he or she has completed recently at school or at home. Remind him or her to use correct verb tenses.

Name ___________________________



# Principal Parts of Regular Verbs

**Directions** Mark the letter of the item that correctly identifies the form of the underlined word or words in each sentence.

**1.** Leonardo had planned a new project.
**A** present
**B** present participle
**C** past
**D** past participle

**2.** This surprised no one.
**A** present
**B** present participle
**C** past
**D** past participle

**3.** He pursued a wide range of interests.
**A** present
**B** present participle
**C** past
**D** past participle

**4.** New ideas distracted him from projects.
**A** present
**B** present participle
**C** past
**D** past participle

**5.** Some have observed that he possessed too many abilities.
**A** present
**B** present participle
**C** past
**D** past participle

**6.** One lifetime contains too few hours for such a man.
**A** present
**B** present participle
**C** past
**D** past participle

**7.** The journals of Leonardo have preserved many of his plans and ideas.
**A** present
**B** present participle
**C** past
**D** past participle

**8.** This is how we learn of his great genius today.
**A** present
**B** present participle
**C** past
**D** past participle

**9.** In them he recorded plans for many inventions.
**A** present
**B** present participle
**C** past
**D** past participle

**10.** We are studying his plan for a flying machine.
**A** present
**B** present participle
**C** past
**D** past participle

**Home Activity** Your child prepared for taking tests on principal parts of verbs. Ask your child to name the principal parts of the verbs *paint* and *invent* and then use each part in a sentence.

Name ______________________

# Principal Parts of Regular Verbs

**Directions** Write *present, present participle, past,* or *past participle* to identify the form of the underlined verb.

1. Machines existed in Leonardo's day. ______
2. For example, water wheels turned millstones. ______
3. As a boy, Leonardo had watched machines closely. ______
4. By adulthood, he had analyzed how each part worked. ______
5. Unlike others, Leonardo combined parts in new ways. ______
6. He thought, "Aha! This change improves the machine!" ______
7. He reasoned, "This invention is working better with different parts." ______
8. He explained his analyses in journals. ______
9. Grateful engineers still study his sketches. ______
10. These illustrations are serving as blueprints for us. ______

**Directions** Write the sentence using the principal part of the underlined verb indicated in ( ).

11. Leonardo refuse all meat. (past)
______
12. He always love animals. (past participle)
______
13. Vegetarians still follow his habit. (present).
______
14. I stop eating meat too. (past participle)
______
15. Fruits and vegetables provide plenty of nutrition. (present)
______

**Home Activity** Your child reviewed principal parts of regular verbs. Have your child identify examples of the use of present, past, and past participle forms in an article or a familiar book.

# Principal Parts of Irregular Verbs

Usually you add *-ed* to a verb to show past tense. **Irregular verbs** do not follow this rule. Instead of having *-ed* forms to show past tense, irregular verbs usually change to other words.

**Present Tense** The king sees the Crystal Palace.
**Present Participle** The king is seeing the Crystal Palace.
**Past Tense** The king saw the Crystal Palace.
**Past Participle** The king has seen the Crystal Palace.

| Present Tense | Present Participle | Past Tense | Past Participle |
|---|---|---|---|
| bring | (am, is, are) bringing | brought | (*has, have, had*) brought |
| build | (am, is, are) building | built | (*has, have, had*) built |
| choose | (am, is, are) choosing | chose | (*has, have, had*) chosen |
| come | (am, is, are) coming | came | (*has, have, had*) come |
| draw | (am, is, are) drawing | drew | (*has, have, had*) drawn |
| eat | (am, is, are) eating | ate | (*has, have, had*) eaten |
| find | (am, is, are) finding | found | (*has, have, had*) found |
| grow | (am, is, are) growing | grew | (*has, have, had*) grown |
| run | (am, is, are) running | ran | (*has, have, had*) run |
| set | (am, is, are) setting | set | (*has, have, had*) set |
| speak | (am, is, are) speaking | spoke | (*has, have, had*) spoken |
| tell | (am, is, are) telling | told | (*has, have, had*) told |

**Directions** Underline the verb in each sentence. Write *present, present participle, past,* or *past participle* to identify the principal part of the verb.

1. He built a studio in Manhattan. ____________________

2. Hawkins had chosen Central Park for his display. ____________________

**Directions** Write the sentence using the principal part of the underlined verb indicated in ( ).

3. Archaeologists find many more dinosaur bones. (past participle)

______________________________________________

4. Today dinosaur exhibits draw huge crowds. (present participle)

______________________________________________

**Home Activity** Your child learned about principal parts of irregular verbs. Ask your child to write the principal parts of *tell* and *write* and then use each part in a sentence telling what he or she could communicate about dinosaurs.

Name ________________________________

# Principal Parts of Irregular Verbs

**Directions** Write a complete sentence using the past participle form of the verb in ( ) with *has* or *have*.

**1.** Mr. Hancock (run) the museum for five years.

______________________________________________

**2.** He (choose) May as membership drive month .

______________________________________________

**3.** He (speak) to many organizations.

______________________________________________

**4.** The membership list (grow) quite large.

______________________________________________

**5.** Mr. Hancock (do) it!

______________________________________________

**6.** The new dinosaur education wing (draw) new members.

______________________________________________

**Directions** Write a paragraph about dinosaurs. Include some past and past participle forms of such irregular verbs as *be, find, come, know,* and *think.*

______________________________________________

______________________________________________

______________________________________________

______________________________________________

______________________________________________

______________________________________________

______________________________________________

______________________________________________

______________________________________________

**Home Activity** Your child learned how to write principal parts of irregular verbs correctly. Ask your child to write about a favorite prehistoric animal. Encourage him or her to use forms of *become, is, see, think, go,* and *eat* when writing.

Name ______________________________

# Principal Parts of Irregular Verbs

**Directions** Mark the letter of the item that correctly identifies the form of the underlined word or words in each sentence.

**1.** A sculptor is building a clay figure.
**A** past
**B** present
**C** past participle
**D** present participle

**2.** She makes a mold of the clay shape.
**A** past
**B** present
**C** past participle
**D** present participle

**3.** She chooses a metal for the mold.
**A** past
**B** present
**C** past participle
**D** present participle

**4.** Many sculptures have begun this way.
**A** past
**B** present
**C** past participle
**D** present participle

**5.** The critics have spoken.
**A** past
**B** present
**C** past participle
**D** present participle

**6.** I saw a wonderful statue.
**A** past
**B** present
**C** past participle
**D** present participle

**7.** He has bought several works by that sculptor.
**A** past
**B** present
**C** past participle
**D** present participle

**8.** I have chosen the artwork I want to buy.
**A** past
**B** present
**C** past participle
**D** present participle

**9.** Set the painting here.
**A** past
**B** present
**C** past participle
**D** present participle

**10.** Who is bringing picture hangers?
**A** past
**B** present
**C** past participle
**D** present participle

**Home Activity** Your child prepared for taking tests on principal parts of irregular verbs. Ask your child to name the principal parts of the verbs *choose* and *find* and then use each part in a sentence.

Name ______________________

# Principal Parts of Irregular Verbs

**Directions** Write *present, present participle, past,* or *past participle* to identify the underlined verb form.

1. The diners eat for eight hours. ______
2. Each diner has told at least one story. ______
3. Hawkins chose the iguanodon model. ______
4. He had set a dining table inside it. ______
5. His guests become excited. ______
6. Hawkins thought they would be. ______
7. The guests told about this event for years. ______
8. The dinosaur fad had begun. ______
9. Today we find Hawkins's models odd. ______
10. We are making more discoveries about dinosaurs. ______

**Directions** Write the sentence using the principal part of the underlined verb indicated in ( ).

11. We know a great deal about the past. (present)

______

12. In 1850, scientists know much less. (past)

______

13. They find some fossils of dinosaur bones. (past participle)

______

14. Sometimes animals freeze in glaciers. (present)

______

15. Explorers find the remains of these animals. (present participle)

______

16. A little of Earth's history freeze with them. (past participle)

______

**Home Activity** Your child reviewed principal parts of irregular verbs. Have your child identify examples of the use of present, present participle, past, and past participle forms in a cookbook or history book.

Name ________________________

# Troublesome Verbs

Some pairs of verbs are confusing because they have similar meanings or because they look alike.

| | Present | Past | Past Participle |
|---|---|---|---|
| *Lay* means "put" or "place." | lay | laid | (*has, have, had*) laid |
| *Lie* means "rest" or "recline." | lie | lay | (*has, have, had*) lain |
| *Set* means "put something somewhere." | set | set | (*has, have, had*) set |
| *Sit* means "sit down." | sit | sat | (*has, have, had*) sat |
| *Let* means "allow." | let | let | (*has, have, had*) let |
| *Leave* means "go away." | leave | left | (*has, have, had*) left |

**Directions** Write the form of the underlined verb indicated in ( ).

1. A teenage girl sit with the choir. (past) ____________
2. She has lay her hand over her heart. (past participle) ____________
3. The choir director let her join. (past) ____________
4. The music never leave her head. (past) ____________
5. When she set her suitcases down in Chicago, Mahalia knew she was home. (past) ____________
6. Mahalia's father had let her follow her dream. (past participle) ____________

**Directions** Use context to help you decide which verb is needed. Then find the principal part needed on the chart. Underline the verb that correctly completes the sentence.

7. I (set, sit) a CD on the counter.
8. Will you (leave, let) me pay for it?
9. My parents have already (left, let) the store.
10. After dinner we (sat, set) down and listened to the CD.
11. Tom has (laid, lain) down on the floor.
12. Fiona (laid, lied) a log on the fire.

**Home Activity** Your child learned about troublesome verbs. Ask your child to explain the difference in meaning between *sit/set, lie/lay,* and *leave/let* and then act out the meanings of the verbs in each pair to demonstrate the difference.

Name ______________________________

# Troublesome Verbs

**Directions** Choose the form of the underlined verb indicated in ( ). Use the chart to help you. Write the sentence on the line.

| Present | Past | Past Participle |
| --- | --- | --- |
| lie ("to rest," "to recline") | lay | (has, have, had) lain |
| lay ("to put," "to place") | laid | (has, have, had) laid |

1. Wes lay the sheet music on the shelf. (past)

______________________________

2. The twins lie beside the pool relaxing. (past)

______________________________

3. Their towels lie on the concrete all day. (past participle)

______________________________

4. We lay the groundwork for next year's concert. (past participle)

______________________________

5. In this song, lay the heaviest emphasis on long vowels. (present)

______________________________

6. The secret lie in hours of practice. (present)

______________________________

**Directions** Write a paragraph describing a photograph of your family or friends. Use as many principal parts of *sit, set, lie, lay, leave,* and *let* as you can.

______________________________

______________________________

______________________________

______________________________

______________________________

______________________________

______________________________

**Home Activity** Your child learned how to write principal parts of troublesome verbs correctly. Ask your child to write sentences about cleaning a room. Encourage him or her to use forms of *lie, lay, sit, set, leave,* and *let*.

Name ____________________



# Troublesome Verbs

**Directions** Mark the letter of the verb that correctly completes each sentence.

**1.** I ____ on the couch last night.
**A** lie
**B** lay
**C** laid
**D** lain

**2.** I usually ____ in this chair.
**A** sit
**B** set
**C** has sat
**D** setted

**3.** The bus has ____ already.
**A** leave
**B** let
**C** left
**D** leaved

**4.** The brickmason has ____ stones in concrete.
**A** sit
**B** set
**C** sat
**D** sitted

**5.** The driver has ____ her keys on the seat.
**A** lie
**B** lay
**C** laid
**D** lain

**6.** He doesn't ____ riders get out of their seats.
**A** leave
**B** let
**C** left
**D** letted

**7.** Betty has ____ in bed all week.
**A** lay
**B** lie
**C** laid
**D** lain

**8.** ____ the area at once!
**A** Leave
**B** Let
**C** Left
**D** Leaved

**9.** Who ____ on my hat?
**A** sit
**B** set
**C** sat
**D** sitted

**10.** The cats always ____ in a sunny spot.
**A** lied
**B** lie
**C** laid
**D** lain

**Home Activity** Your child prepared for taking tests on principal parts of troublesome verbs. Ask your child to name the principal parts of the verbs *lie, lay, sit, set, leave,* and *let* and then use each part in a sentence.

Name ______________________________

# Troublesome Verbs

**Directions** Write the letter of the definition of the underlined verb.

_____ **1.** You left without your music.
_____ **2.** She had set it on the piano.
_____ **3.** Lay the tickets on the counter.
_____ **4.** I sit and listen to the players.
_____ **5.** Joan has lain in the sun too long.
_____ **6.** Tim has not let that bother him.

**A** am seated
**B** has allowed
**C** has rested or reclined
**D** went away
**E** place or put
**F** had put (a thing) somewhere

**Directions** Choose a verb from the box to complete each sentence. Write the sentence on the line.

| lay | leave | let | lain | sit | set |
|---|---|---|---|---|---|

**7.** __________ the oven at 350º before you leave.

______________________________________________

**8.** Everyone, please __________ at the table.

______________________________________________

**9.** Mom and Dad __________ for their voice lesson at 7:15.

______________________________________________

**10.** They __________ us fix our own dinner.

______________________________________________

**Directions** Underline the verb that correctly completes the sentence.

**11.** I have (laid, lain) in a hammock.

**12.** Yesterday you (sat, set) up front.

**13.** The music teacher (left, let) the room.

**14.** First she (laid, lain) the chalk on the desk.

**Home Activity** Your child reviewed principal parts of troublesome verbs. Have your child write a joke using different forms of *sit, set, lie, lay, leave,* and *let* correctly.

Name ______________________________

# Prepositions and Prepositional Phrases

A **preposition** begins a group of words called a **prepositional phrase**. The noun or pronoun that follows the preposition is called the **object of the preposition**. Prepositional phrases provide details about the rest of the sentence.

People have watched animated movies for a long time. (preposition)
People have watched animated movies for a long time. (prepositional phrase)
People have watched animated movies for a long time. (object of the preposition)

**Common Prepositions**

| | | | | | |
|---|---|---|---|---|---|
| about | around | by | into | over | until |
| above | at | down | near | through | up |
| across | before | for | of | to | with |
| after | below | from | on | toward | |
| against | between | in | onto | under | |

**Directions** Underline the prepositional phrase in each sentence. Write *P* above the preposition. Write *O* above the object of the preposition.

**1.** The characters in animated films often seem quite real.

**2.** Young viewers may identify with the superheroes.

**3.** Ariel was a mermaid who lived under the sea.

**4.** She wanted a life on dry land.

**5.** Her father was Neptune, king of the sea.

**Directions** Underline the prepositional phrases. The number in ( ) tells how many prepositional phrases are in that sentence.

**6.** Many fairy tales have been made into animated movies for children. (2)

**7.** Their stories take youngsters from childhood into adulthood. (2)

**8.** The hero of the tale must pass through trials and adventures. (2)

**9.** At the end, he or she has shown great strength of character. (2)

**Home Activity** Your child learned about prepositions and prepositional phrases. Read a favorite story with your child. Ask him or her to point out prepositional phrases and identify the preposition and object of the preposition in each.

Name ______________________________

# Prepositions and Prepositional Phrases

**Directions** Add a preposition to complete each sentence. Write the sentence on the line.

**1.** I usually lie __________ the floor when I watch TV.

______________________________

**2.** When I get hungry, I get a snack __________ the refrigerator.

______________________________

**3.** We have several movies stored __________ the television.

______________________________

**4.** I would rather see a movie __________ the theater.

______________________________

**5.** The big screen and the smell __________ popcorn create a memorable experience.

______________________________

**Directions** Add a prepositional phrase of your own to complete each sentence. Write the sentence.

**6.** Let's make Dad a cartoon __________.

______________________________

**7.** I'll get the paper and markers __________.

______________________________

**8.** You draw the scenes in pencil, and I'll color them __________.

______________________________

**9.** What colors shall we use __________?

______________________________

**10.** Dad will hang this cartoon __________.

______________________________

**Home Activity** Your child learned how to use prepositions and prepositional phrases in writing. Ask your child to write about his or her favorite animated film using at least one prepositional phrase in each sentence.

Name ______________________________

# Subject and Object Pronouns

A **subject pronoun** is used in the subject of a sentence. Singular subject pronouns are *I, you, he, she,* and *it*. Plural subject pronouns are *we, you,* and *they*. When you use a person's name and a pronoun in a compound subject, be sure to use a subject pronoun.

He has many original ideas. They are exciting and unusual.
Mom and I made bird feeders.

An **object pronoun** is used in the predicate of a sentence after an action verb or with a preposition, such as *for, at, into, with,* or *to*. Singular object pronouns are *me, you, him, her,* and *it*. Plural object pronouns are *us, you,* and *them*. When you use a person's name and a pronoun in a compound object, be sure to use an object pronoun.

The teacher asked him about his project. It seemed brilliant to me.
This project was fun for James and me.

**Directions** Write *S* if the underlined word is a subject pronoun. Write *O* if the word is an object pronoun.

1. Some kids don't know what to think about him. ______
2. They can't understand someone who is different from them. ______
3. She praised his project for its originality. ______
4. Rainelle and I invited him to sit with us. ______
5. We were fascinated by his ideas. ______
6. He has become a valued friend to her and me. ______

**Directions** Underline the correct pronoun in ( ) to complete each sentence.

7. Most people choose friends who are like (them, they).
8. (Them, They) feel comfortable with people who agree with them.
9. You and (I, me) have different points of view.
10. A friend with original ideas always surprises (I, me).
11. (Us, We) need to think about what we do and say.
12. (I, Me) prefer independent thinkers.
13. Jose and (her, she) agree with me.
14. We have many exciting conversations with (he, him) and (she, her).

**Home Activity** Your child learned about subject and object pronouns. Read a magazine article with your child. Ask him or her to identify several subject pronouns and object pronouns in the article.

Name ______________________________

# Subject and Object Pronouns

**Directions** Use a pronoun from the box to complete each sentence. Write the sentence.

| they | he | I | us |
|---|---|---|---|
| them | she | me | you |

**1.** My mom and ______________ plant a garden every summer.

**2.** ______________ lets me pick out the seeds we will plant.

**3.** Some new flowers surprised ______________ both this season.

**4.** ______________ looked very strange among the roses and daisies.

**5.** As we watched ______________ grow, we became more and more amazed.

**6.** Their enormous leaves and huge white flowers puzzled ______________ and Mom.

**7.** Finally, Dad confessed. ______________ had planted moonflower seeds to surprise us!

**8.** Would ______________ have fallen for his joke?

**Directions** Write a paragraph about a unique person you know. Use subject and object pronouns correctly.

______________________________________________________________________

______________________________________________________________________

______________________________________________________________________

______________________________________________________________________

______________________________________________________________________

______________________________________________________________________

______________________________________________________________________

______________________________________________________________________

______________________________________________________________________

______________________________________________________________________

______________________________________________________________________

**Home Activity** Your child learned how to use subject and object pronouns in writing. Ask your child to write a description of something he or she did with a friend or a group. Remind your child to use subject and object pronouns correctly.

Name ______________________

# Subject and Object Pronouns

**Directions** Mark the letter of the pronoun that correctly completes each sentence.

**1.** ____ like to find wild foods.
**A** Them
**B** I
**C** Me
**D** She

**2.** You can make a meal of ____.
**A** we
**B** they
**C** them
**D** he

**3.** Dana and ____ found wild strawberries.
**A** he
**B** him
**C** us
**D** them

**4.** In the fall ____ harvest cattails.
**A** me
**B** her
**C** us
**D** they

**5.** ____ can grind the roots to make flour.
**A** Him
**B** We
**C** Them
**D** Her

**6.** Papa and ____ hunt for mushrooms in the woods.
**A** her
**B** me
**C** she
**D** us

**7.** Have ____ ever picked wild asparagus?
**A** you
**B** it
**C** them
**D** him

**8.** Uncle Dick and ____ found hickory nuts.
**A** us
**B** her
**C** them
**D** they

**9.** Dad asked Phil and ____ to shell the nuts.
**A** she
**B** he
**C** me
**D** I

**10.** He and ____ agreed it is a messy job.
**A** them
**B** I
**C** it
**D** her

**Home Activity** Your child prepared for taking tests on subject and object pronouns. Have your child write subject pronouns and object pronouns on index cards. Then mix the cards and sort them into subject pronoun and object pronoun piles.

Name ______________________________



# Subject and Object Pronouns

**Directions** Write the letter of each pronoun next to the correct category.

______ **1.** Singular subject pronoun — **A** we

______ **2.** Plural object pronoun — **B** she

______ **3.** Singular object pronoun — **C** me

______ **4.** Plural subject pronoun — **D** you

______ **5.** Singular and plural, subject and object pronoun — **E** them

**Directions** Write *S* if the underlined word is a subject pronoun. Write *O* if the word is an object pronoun.

**6.** We learned about the Anasazi people. ______

**7.** They built a civilization in the Southwest. ______

**8.** Like many civilizations, it depended on crops. ______

**9.** Maize and pumpkins provided the staple foods for them. ______

**10.** Little rain fell, but the Anasazi hoarded it to water crops. ______

**11.** The teacher asked Lia and me to report on cliff dwellings. ______

**Directions** Underline the correct pronoun in ( ) to complete each sentence.

**12.** My family and (I, me) visited Chaco Canyon.

**13.** (Us, We) learned about the pueblos the Anasazi built there.

**14.** Their skill in building with adobe amazed Sara and (I, me).

**15.** The people who lived here disappeared 800 years ago and took little with (them, they).

**16.** Why they left is a mystery to (us, we).

**17.** Scientists and (they, them) agree that drought may have forced them to migrate.

**Home Activity** Your child reviewed subject and object pronouns. Challenge your child to write sentences using *you, he, she, it, him, her,* and *them* correctly.

Name ______________________________

# Pronouns and Antecedents

A **pronoun** takes the place of a noun or nouns. An **antecedent**, or referent, is the noun or nouns to which the pronoun refers. A pronoun and its antecedent must agree in number and gender.

Before you use a pronoun, ask yourself whether the antecedent is singular or plural. If the antecedent is singular, decide whether it is masculine, feminine, or neuter. Then choose a pronoun that agrees. In the following sentences, the antecedents are underlined once; the pronouns are underlined twice.

Charlie participates in tennis and track for exercise. They keep him in shape.

**Directions** Circle the correct pronoun or pronouns in ( ) to complete each sentence. The antecedent of each pronoun is underlined to help you.

**1.** Will loves tennis because (it, he) takes strength and speed.

**2.** Iris practices figure skating, and (they, she) is good at it.

**3.** The twins play baseball, but bowling interests (them, they) too.

**4.** Exercise makes people feel good because (it, they) keeps (she, them) fit.

**5.** José lost strength when (he, him) broke his leg.

**6.** The physical therapist showed José exercises that helped (he, him).

**Directions** Underline the antecedent once and the pronoun twice in each sentence.

**7.** An English doctor wrote about a disorder he observed in many children.

**8.** The children had stiff muscles, so moving was difficult for them.

**9.** As these children grew up, the condition did not grow worse, nor did it grow better.

**10.** Dr. William Little made the discovery, and he named the disorder Little's disease.

**11.** Several disorders are called cerebral palsy, and Little's disease is one of them.

**12.** A girl with cerebral palsy will have difficulty when she tries to move about.

**Home Activity** Your child learned about pronouns and antecedents. Read a magazine article together and have your child find pronouns that have antecedents and identify both.

Name ____________________

# Pronouns and Antecedents

**Directions** Write a sentence or a pair of sentences using the noun or noun phrase and pronoun. Use each noun as an antecedent of each pronoun.

**1.** Kids with CP/they

**2.** exercise/it

**3.** strong muscles/them

**4.** physical therapist/he

**5.** girl with CP/her

**Directions** Write a paragraph about someone who works hard to overcome a physical handicap. Use at least four pronouns with their antecedents. Underline the antecedent for each pronoun.

**Home Activity** Your child learned how to use pronouns and antecedents in writing. With your child, write a paragraph about a hard worker you admire. Have your child point out pronouns and underline their antecedents.

Name ______________________________

# Pronouns and Antecedents

**Directions** Read the following paragraph. Mark the letter of the pronoun that correctly completes each sentence.

**(1)** Carlie is my newest cousin; ____ was born in June. **(2)** Mom, Dad, and I drove to the hospital so ____ could see her. **(3)** There were six babies in the nursery; ____ were all sleeping. **(4)** When a baby is born, ____ is checked carefully. **(5)** If there is any problem, doctors want to catch ____ right away. **(6)** For example, heart and lungs are checked to make sure ____ are functioning normally. **(7)** Carlie's doctor examined ____ and reported that everything is fine. **(8)** When my cousin Jimmy was born, ____ had a heart murmur. **(9)** Doctors operated on ____ and corrected the problem. **(10)** Parents always say that for ____, the main thing is having a happy, healthy baby.

**1.** **A** she **B** her **C** they **D** him

**2.** **A** he **B** they **C** us **D** we

**3.** **A** them **B** they **C** she **D** he

**4.** **A** him **B** her **C** it **D** them

**5.** **A** they **B** it **C** she **D** her

**6.** **A** they **B** it **C** them **D** we

**7.** **A** she **B** her **C** them **D** they

**8.** **A** him **B** he **C** it **D** them

**9.** **A** him **B** he **C** she **D** her

**10.** **A** she **B** he **C** they **D** them

**Home Activity** Your child prepared for taking tests on pronouns and antecedents. Have your child rewrite a paragraph from a story, replacing each pronoun with its antecedent. Ask him or her to explain why pronouns make the story sound better.

Name ______________________________

# Pronouns and Antecedents

**Directions** Match the pronoun with the noun or noun phrase that could be its antecedent. Write the letter of the correct antecedent next to the pronoun.

______ **1.** she  **A** boys and girls

______ **2.** them  **B** Mr. Zimmerman

______ **3.** it  **C** Grandpa and I

______ **4.** we  **D** the prize

______ **5.** he  **E** Susan

**Directions** Circle the antecedent of the underlined pronoun in each sentence.

**6.** When muscles contract, they shorten.

**7.** A voluntary muscle contracts when you want it to.

**8.** Involuntary muscles are controlled by your brain. You do not tell them what to do.

**9.** The heart is an involuntary muscle, so it works automatically.

**10.** Leila explained how she slows her heart rate by relaxing.

**Directions** Write a pronoun to replace each underlined noun or noun phrase.

**11.** When people think of movement, people think of muscle power.

______________________

**12.** A muscle is vital to moving the body, but a muscle is only part of the story.

______________________

**13.** The bones are the other part. Bones move the body when muscles contract and pull on bones.

______________________

**14.** Carole flexed her arm, and Carole felt her bicep muscle contract.

______________________

**15.** Sean exclaimed, "Sean can see the muscles working in pairs! One contracts and the other relaxes."

______________________

**Home Activity** Your child reviewed pronouns and antecedents. Have your child dictate sentences about how he or she used muscles today. Ask your child to underline pronouns and circle any antecedents in the sentences.

Name ______________________

# Possessive Pronouns

**Possessive pronouns** show who or what owns, or possesses, something. *My, mine, your, yours, her, hers, his, its, our, ours, their,* and *theirs* are possessive pronouns.

- Use *my, your, her, our,* and *their* before nouns.
  Is that your cat? It was her gerbil. They pet our dog.
- Use *mine, yours, hers, ours,* and *theirs* alone.
  The cat is yours. That gerbil is hers. The dog is ours.
- *His* and *its* can be used both before nouns and alone.
  He lost his ferret. The ferret is his.
  The dog lost its collar. The collar is its.
- Do not use an apostrophe with a possessive pronoun.

**Directions** Replace the underlined words or phrases with possessive pronouns. Rewrite the sentences.

**1.** An ant colony relies on the ant colony's queen.

______________________

______________________

**2.** Both males and females have wings on the males' and females' bodies.

______________________

______________________

**3.** The queen ant flies to a new location to start a colony, then sheds the queen's wings.

______________________

______________________

**4.** Ants are very strong for ants' size and can carry 25 times ants' weight.

______________________

______________________

**5.** Most of us think that ants are pests to be swept out of most of us's way.

______________________

______________________

**Home Activity** Your child learned about possessive pronouns. Ask your child to make up sentences about objects at home that belong to him or her, to the family, and to others. Have your child identify the possessive pronouns he or she uses.

Name ____________________

# Possessive Pronouns

**Directions** Underline the error in each sentence. Write the correct possessive pronoun in the space above the error.

**(1)** Each animal is adapted to it's environment. **(2)** For example, snakes have temperature-sensing organs on they're heads. **(3)** They can use these organs to locate there prey in the dark. **(4)** My corn snake Lolamae can take a whole mouse or egg in hers mouth. **(5)** She can unhinge her's bottom jaw to fit in a big meal. **(6)** The aquarium in the corner is her. **(7)** Lolamae will be happy to slither up yours arm. **(8)** It took mine mom a long time to get used to Lolamae too.

**Directions** Write a paragraph about pets you and your friends have owned. Describe some unique features of the pets. Use at least five possessive pronouns. Underline the possessive pronouns in your paragraph.

____________________

____________________

____________________

____________________

____________________

____________________

____________________

____________________

____________________

____________________

____________________

____________________

____________________

**Home Activity** Your child learned how to use possessive pronouns in writing. Have your child write interview questions to ask you about a prized possession and then write your answers below the questions.

Name ______________________

# Possessive Pronouns

**Directions** Write the letter of the possessive pronoun that correctly completes each sentence in the paragraph.

**(1)** Last night I heard a haunting sound outside ____ window. **(2)** My brother and I ran into ____ yard to find out what it was. **(3)** He shined ____ flashlight up into a tree. **(4)** We saw two big eyes, and ____ unblinking stare unnerved me. **(5)** It was only a screech owl, but ____ hoot sounded eerie. **(6)** Since that night, owls have become a hobby of ____. **(7)** Mom loaned me some of ____ biology books. **(8)** Did you know that owls can turn ____ heads almost completely around? **(9)** This is an adaptation of ____ that allows them to turn their heads to follow a moving object. **(10)** Now Mom and I spend ____ free time on weekends bird watching.

**1.** **A** mine
**B** my
**C** theirs
**D** hers

**2.** **A** her
**B** hers
**C** our
**D** theirs

**3.** **A** mine
**B** his
**C** its
**D** their

**4.** **A** your
**B** its
**C** their
**D** theirs

**5.** **A** theirs
**B** its
**C** hers
**D** her

**6.** **A** mine
**B** our
**C** their
**D** it's

**7.** **A** hers
**B** her
**C** their
**D** theirs

**8.** **A** our
**B** her
**C** their
**D** my

**9.** **A** hers
**B** his
**C** their
**D** theirs

**10.** **A** mine
**B** my
**C** ours
**D** our

**Home Activity** Your child prepared for taking tests on possessive pronouns. Have your child choose a magazine article and find possessive pronouns in it. Ask him or her to name the person or thing each possessive pronoun stands for.

Name ______________________________

# Possessive Pronouns

**Directions** Write the letter of the possessive pronoun that can replace the underlined word or words in each phrase.

| | | |
|---|---|---|
| _____ | **1.** Aaron's and Mike's question | **A** her |
| _____ | **2.** Mr. Shaefer's lesson | **B** their |
| _____ | **3.** the book's index | **C** our |
| _____ | **4.** Sam's and my interest | **D** its |
| _____ | **5.** Mom's degree | **E** his |

**Directions** Underline the pronoun that correctly completes each sentence.

**6.** We will catch fireflies in (theirs, our) hands.

**7.** Which of these jars is (your, yours)?

**8.** Be sure to punch air holes in (it's, its) top.

**9.** Dusk is (their, theirs) time to glow and flash.

**10.** I have ten fireflies in (my, mine) jar.

**11.** The light flashes from (their, it's) abdomen.

**12.** We let the fireflies go. Our friends released (their, theirs) later.

**Directions** Write the possessive pronoun that can replace the underlined word or words.

**13.** A snake sheds a snake's skin when it outgrows it.

______________________

**14.** This bleached-out turtle shell is the one belonging to me.

______________________

**15.** Zara and Ted explained that the rat was Zara's and the hamster was Ted's.

______________________

**Home Activity** Your child reviewed possessive pronouns. Ask your child to list the possessive pronouns on this page, use each one in an example sentence, and tell you what possessive noun the possessive pronoun replaces.

Name ______________________________

# Indefinite and Reflexive Pronouns

**Indefinite pronouns** may not refer to specific words. They do not have definite antecedents.
Someone called and left a message.

Some common indefinite pronouns are listed below.

| Singular Indefinite Pronouns | Plural Indefinite Pronouns |
| --- | --- |
| someone, somebody, anyone, anybody, everyone, everybody, something, no one, either, each | few, several, both, others, many all, some |

- Use singular verb forms with singular indefinite pronouns and plural verb forms with plural indefinite pronouns: Everyone feels lonely at times. Others offer them friendship.

**Reflexive pronouns** reflect the action of the verb back on the subject. Reflexive pronouns end in *-self* or *-selves*: Vic wrote a note to himself.

| Singular Reflexive Pronouns | Plural Reflexive Pronouns |
| --- | --- |
| himself, herself, myself, itself, yourself | ourselves, yourselves, themselves |

- There are no such words as *hisself, theirself, theirselves,* or *ourself.*

**Directions** Underline the correct pronoun in ( ) to complete each sentence.

1. (Anyone, Many) benefits by making new friends.
2. (Many, Anyone) treasure old friends too.
3. My friends and I taught (ourself, ourselves) chess.
4. We play in the cafeteria, but (few, no one) know this.
5. (Everyone, Others) is welcome to join us.
6. A new student introduced (himself, hisself).
7. (Some, Someone) calls him Dylan.
8. (Something, Many) tells me Dylan has learned chess from a master.
9. We know the moves, but he knows the game (itself, themselves).
10. (Someone, Others) tell me I'm good at chess, but Dylan beat me.
11. I hope Dylan enjoyed (herself, himself) today.
12. You should learn chess (ourself, yourself)

**Home Activity** Your child learned about indefinite and reflexive pronouns. Ask your child to make up several statements about making friends using pronouns such as *everybody, no one, many, few,* and *myself*.

Name ______________________

# Indefinite and Reflexive Pronouns

| ourselves | everyone | yourself | few |
|---|---|---|---|
| myself | anyone | herself | both |

**Directions** Choose a pronoun from the box to complete each sentence correctly. Be sure indefinite pronouns used as subjects agree in number with their verbs.

1. "Tell us about ____________, Tonya," says the teacher.
2. I think to ____________, "This is going to be good!"
3. ____________ leans forward to listen.
4. Tonya is a cowgirl who taught ____________ to ride.
5. ____________ of us know anything at all about horses.
6. Tonya says that ____________ can ride her gentle horse Bluebonnet.
7. All of us think to ____________, "I might not be able to!"
8. My friend Tonya has two horses, and ____________ are beautiful.

**Directions** Write several sentences about a time you made a new friend. Use some indefinite and reflexive pronouns. Underline the indefinite and reflexive pronouns you use.

______________________________________________

______________________________________________

______________________________________________

______________________________________________

______________________________________________

______________________________________________

______________________________________________

______________________________________________

______________________________________________

______________________________________________

______________________________________________

______________________________________________

**Home Activity** Your child learned how to write indefinite and reflexive pronouns. Have your child write these pronouns on cards. Choose several cards at a time and ask him or her to write sentences using the pronouns.

Name ______________________________

# Indefinite and Reflexive Pronouns

**Directions** Mark the letter of the pronoun that correctly completes each sentence.

**1.** This alarm clock turns ____ off.
**A** themself
**B** itself
**C** herself
**D** yourself

**2.** ____ lets the dog out at 3.
**A** Someone
**B** Many
**C** Something
**D** Few

**3.** ____ is welcome to try out.
**A** Themselves
**B** Others
**C** Anyone
**D** Many

**4.** Marla taught ____ to sing.
**A** itself
**B** themselves
**C** himself
**D** herself

**5.** ____ sends us a mystery package every year.
**A** Himself
**B** Somebody
**C** Both
**D** Several

**6.** ____ likes getting a shot.
**A** Myself
**B** Few
**C** No one
**D** Many

**7.** Sam bought ____ a watch.
**A** itself
**B** themself
**C** himself
**D** hisself

**8.** ____ is wrong.
**A** Myself
**B** Something
**C** Itself
**D** Others

**9.** May we help ____?
**A** ourself
**B** themself
**C** hisself
**D** ourselves

**10.** ____ volunteer for safety patrol duty.
**A** Many
**B** No one
**C** Everyone
**D** Someone

**Home Activity** Your child prepared for taking tests on indefinite and reflexive pronouns. Have your child write each indefinite and reflexive pronoun on an index card. Mix the cards and have your child sort them by type and number.

Name ________________________________

# Indefinite and Reflexive Pronouns

**Directions** Underline the pronoun in each sentence. Write *indefinite* or *reflexive* to identify the kind of pronoun it is. Then write *singular* or *plural* to show its number.

1. Everyone wants friends. ________________ ________________
2. Anna told herself to smile. ________________ ________________
3. A smile multiplies itself. ________________ ________________
4. Many begin to smile at Anna. ________________ ________________
5. Anybody can give a smile. ________________ ________________

**Directions** Underline the correct pronoun in ( ) to complete each sentence.

6. (Someone, Both) are friendly.
7. (Everyone, Many) agrees they are good friends
8. (No one, Others) are welcome in our club.
9. (Several, Anybody) have inquired about joining.
10. The boys signed (himself, themselves) up for bowling class.
11. (Anybody, Yourself) can try out for the class play.
12. Marcus and I practiced our parts by (himself, ourselves).

**Directions** Choose a pronoun from the box to complete each sentence correctly. Be sure indefinite pronouns used as subjects agree in number with their verbs.

| ourselves | everybody | themselves | few |
|---|---|---|---|

13. ________________ in class was to choose an after-school activity.
14. A ________________ of us are signing up for poetry.
15. Ms. Lonway will let us choose a poet for ________________.
16. Humorous poets don't take ________________ too seriously.

**Home Activity** Your child reviewed indefinite and reflexive pronouns. Have your child reread a favorite story and identify the indefinite and reflexive pronouns in it as singular or plural.

Name ______________________________

# Using *Who* and *Whom*

People sometimes confuse the pronouns *who* and *whom* when they write. *Who* is a subject form. It is used as a subject of a sentence or a clause.

*Who* made this mess?
I saw a performer *who* could do four back flips. [*Who* is the subject in the dependent clause *who could do four back flips*.]

*Whom* is an object form. It is used as the object of a preposition or as a direct object.

To *whom* did you send a letter?
*Whom* will you ask?

In the first example, *whom* is the object of the preposition *to*. In the second example, *whom* is a direct object.

- To understand why *whom* is used in the second sentence, change the word order so that the subject comes first. (*Whom will you ask?* becomes *You will ask whom?*) This makes it easier to see that *whom* is a direct object.

**Directions** How is the underlined word used? Write *subject*, *object of preposition*, or *direct object*.

1. Who wants to learn gymnastics? ______________________
2. She is a person for whom gymnastics is hard. ______________________
3. Matt is the person who did a triple somersault. ______________________
4. Whom did she help the most? ______________________
5. Who won the Olympic medal last year? ______________________

**Directions** Underline *who* or *whom* to complete each sentence correctly.

6. (Who, Whom) should we support?
7. Work with Brenda, (who, whom) has taken gymnastics for years.
8. To (who, whom) should we go for advice?
9. (Who, Whom) remembers the order of events?
10. The gymnast (who, whom) stumbled on the dismount still won a medal.

**Home Activity** Your child learned about using *who* and *whom*. Ask your child to write sentences about a sport using *whom* as an object and *who* as a subject.

Name ______________________________



# Using *Who* and *Whom*

**Directions** Choose *who* or *whom* to correctly complete each sentence. Then write this sentence and answer or explain it with another sentence or two.

**1.** A person who/whom I admire is ____________________.

______________________________

______________________________

______________________________

**2.** To who/whom do I go for advice?

______________________________

______________________________

______________________________

**3.** Who/Whom is my good friend?

______________________________

______________________________

______________________________

**4.** Who/Whom is a person from history I'd like to meet?

______________________________

______________________________

______________________________

**Directions** Write two sentences about a sport you would like to learn and the person whom you would like as a coach. Use *who* or *whom* correctly in each sentence.

**5.** ______________________________

______________________________

**6.** ______________________________

______________________________

**Home Activity** Your child learned how to use *who* and *whom* correctly in writing. Ask him or her to write a fictional news story about sports and use the pronouns *who* and *whom* in it.

Name ______________________________



# Using *Who* and *Whom*

**Directions** Mark the letter of the answer that tells how the underlined word is used.

**1.** That is the teacher whom I like best.
**A** subject
**B** object of preposition
**C** direct object
**D** noun

**2.** Whom will you ask to the party?
**A** direct object
**B** verb
**C** subject
**D** object of preposition

**3.** Janelle asked, "Who can help me?"
**A** object of preposition
**B** adjective
**C** direct object
**D** subject

**4.** She is a gymnast who works hard.
**A** verb
**B** subject
**C** direct object
**D** object of preposition

**5.** For whom should we ask?
**A** noun
**B** subject
**C** object of preposition
**D** direct object

**6.** Everyone to whom she spoke smiled.
**A** object of preposition
**B** subject
**C** direct object
**D** verb

**Directions** Mark the letter of the sentence that is correct.

**7.** **A** Whom has finished the assignment?
**B** By whom was this work done?
**C** He is a teacher whom praises students often.
**D** Who did he choose?

**8.** **A** He helped the students who were having trouble.
**B** To who can I turn this in?
**C** Who did you help?
**D** Whom won the gymnastics award this year?

**9.** **A** The winner is the one to who a trophy is given.
**B** Chele is the partner with who I worked.
**C** He is the judge who gave high marks.
**D** She likes the gymnast whom is short and slim.

**10.** **A** I like gymnasts whom take chances.
**B** Whom was your favorite performer?
**C** I choose someone whom has pluck.
**D** Whom would you choose?

**Home Activity** Your child prepared for taking tests on *who* and *whom*. Have your child read newspaper articles to highlight uses of *who* and *whom*. Then ask him or her to tell whether the words are used correctly, and why.

Name ___________________________

# Using *Who* and *Whom*

**Directions** Write *subject, object of preposition,* or *direct object* to identify how the underlined word is used.

1. To whom did Rosa speak? ______________
2. Who likes tumbling? ______________
3. A gymnast is someone who is agile and strong. ______________
4. The girl with whom Jordan practices has real talent. ______________
5. People who are flexible are better at somersaults. ______________
6. Whom did you choose as a partner? ______________

**Directions** Underline *who* or *whom* to complete each sentence correctly.

7. (Who, Whom) said that gymnastics is easy?
8. No one (who, whom) has studied gymnastics would say that.
9. Harry, (who, whom) I have coached for three years, shows promise.
10. To (who, whom) shall we give the "Most Improved" award?
11. Marla is the gymnast with (who, whom) most teammates want to work.
12. Our grandfather, (who, whom) is now 65, competed on his college gymnastics team.
13. (Who, Whom) will win Olympic gold this year?
14. (Who, Whom) made the banner congratulating the team?

**Directions** Cross out mistakes in the use of *who* and *whom* in the paragraph. Write the correct pronoun above the line.

**(15)** Kids whom live in the same family often compete with each other. **(16)** They want to see who the parents like best. **(17)** Parents, whom love all their children equally, try not to play favorites. **(18)** Although brothers and sisters like to see whom is faster or stronger, they love each other too.

**Home Activity** Your child reviewed using *who* and *whom*. Read a story with your child, and then ask him or her to tell about favorite characters, using *who* and *whom* correctly.

Name ____________________



# Contractions and Negatives

A **contraction** is a shortened form of two words. An **apostrophe** is used to show where one or more letters have been left out. Some contractions are made by combining pronouns and verbs: *I + have = I've; you + are = you're*. Other contractions are formed by joining a verb and *not: should + not = shouldn't; were + not = weren't.*

- *Won't* and *can't* are formed in special ways (*can + not = can't; will + not = won't*).

**Negatives** are words that mean "no" or "not": *no, not, never, none, nothing*. Contractions with *n't* are negatives too. To make a negative statement, use only one negative word.

**No:** Don't never ask about his leg. There won't be none left.
**Yes:** Don't ever ask about his leg. There won't be any left.

- Use positive words instead of the negative in a sentence with *not*:

| Negative | Positive | Negative | Positive |
|---|---|---|---|
| nobody | anybody, somebody | nothing | anything, something |
| no one | anyone, someone | nowhere | anywhere, somewhere |
| none | any, all, some | never | ever, always |

**Directions** Write the letter of the two words used to form each contraction.

_____ **1.** what's — **A** has not

_____ **2.** that'll — **B** that will

_____ **3.** didn't — **C** they are

_____ **4.** hasn't — **D** could not

_____ **5.** they're — **E** did not

_____ **6.** couldn't — **F** what has

**Directions** Write the contraction for each pair of words.

**7.** would + have = ____________ **9.** it + is = ____________

**8.** she + will = ____________ **10.** will + not = ____________

**Directions** Circle the word in ( ) that correctly completes each sentence.

**11.** You can't (never, ever) tell what Grandma will do.

**12.** There wasn't (nobody, anybody) in the sitting room.

**Home Activity** Your child learned about contractions and negatives. With your child, scan articles in the newspaper to find contractions. Ask your child to write the words used to form each contraction.

Name ______________________________

# Contractions and Negatives

**Directions** Use contractions to replace the underlined words. Rewrite the sentences.

**1.** Those who have lived through an earthquake never forget the experience.

______________________________

______________________________

**2.** It is astonishing that the Earth itself can be shaken.

______________________________

**3.** I cannot believe that rock actually bends.

______________________________

**4.** When it has bent too far, it breaks, and the broken surfaces slide past each other.

______________________________

______________________________

**5.** I have not experienced an earthquake.

______________________________

**6.** Most earthquakes are not very strong.

______________________________

**Directions** Rewrite the sentences, correcting any double negatives.

**7.** No one never wants to be surprised by an earthquake.

______________________________

**8.** There isn't nowhere on Earth that is immune from earthquakes.

______________________________

**9.** Scientists haven't found no way to prevent earthquakes.

______________________________

**10.** There weren't no major earthquakes this year in California.

______________________________

**Home Activity** Your child learned how to write negatives and contractions correctly. Ask your child to write a paragraph about a natural disaster, using several contractions and negatives. Have him or her underline these words.

Name ______________________________

# Contractions and Negatives

**Directions** Mark the letter of the contraction that correctly completes each sentence.

**1.** ____ he talk to the press?
**A** Wont
**B** Won't
**C** Willn't
**D** Don't

**2.** ____ quite a story he told!
**A** We've
**B** Its
**C** That'll
**D** That's

**3.** They are glad ____ here.
**A** you're
**B** you'are
**C** your
**D** youre

**4.** ____ been a long time.
**A** Its
**B** Its'
**C** It's
**D** Thats'

**5.** ____ got to go now.
**A** They'll
**B** They
**C** They've
**D** Theyve

**6.** ____ watch the news tonight.
**A** Well
**B** We'll
**C** We'ill
**D** Well'

**Directions** Mark the letter of the words that correctly complete the sentence.

**7.** ____ told you about the interview?
**A** Hasn't no one
**B** Has no one not
**C** Hasn't anyone
**D** Hasn't anyone never

**8.** There ____ at the station.
**A** wasn't anyone
**B** was'nt anyone
**C** wasn't no one
**D** isn't nobody

**9.** The nurse ____ to be seen.
**A** wasn't nowhere
**B** was nowhere
**C** didn't never want
**D** don't want

**10.** Peter said he ____ surprises.
**A** didn't want no
**B** don't want no
**C** doesn't want no
**D** didn't want any

**Home Activity** Your child prepared for taking tests on contractions and negatives. Ask your child to write contractions on one side of index cards and the words used to form them on the other side. Help your child practice identifying them.

Name ______________________________

# Contractions and Negatives

**Directions** Underline the contraction in each sentence. Write the words that make up the contraction.

**1.** I'll make a special birthday gift for Grandma. ____________________

**2.** She says that she doesn't want any gifts. ____________________

**3.** I'd be willing to bet she likes this one. ____________________

**4.** It's a scrapbook about her grandchildren. ____________________

**5.** Won't that make her eyes sparkle? ____________________

**Directions** Draw a line to connect each contraction with the words used to form it.

| | |
|---|---|
| **6.** could've | you are |
| **7.** they'll | it is |
| **8.** who'd | could have |
| **9.** you're | who would |
| **10.** it's | they will |

**Directions** Circle the word in ( ) that correctly completes each sentence.

**11.** Great-Grandfather Lou doesn't (ever, never) want us to forget our history.

**12.** For fifty years, he has (ever, never) missed a day of writing in his diary.

**13.** When I read it, I thought I had never seen (anything, nothing) like it.

**14.** "Grandpa," I said, "there hasn't ever been (anybody, nobody) with as interesting a life as you."

**15.** "Tell me everything," I requested. "Don't leave (anything, nothing) out!"

**Home Activity** Your child reviewed contractions and negatives. Ask him or her to write a story that uses at least five contractions and five negatives correctly. Have your child highlight these words and read you the story.

Name ______________________________

# Adjectives and Articles

An **adjective** describes a noun or pronoun. It tells what kind, how many, or which one.

| | |
|---|---|
| **What Kind** | a gigantic white iceberg |
| **How Many** | numerous icebergs; several chances |
| **Which One** | this lifeboat |

The **articles** *a, an,* and *the* appear before nouns or other adjectives.

- Use **a** before words that begin with a consonant sound: a disaster, a rapid speed.
- Use **an** before words that begin with a vowel sound or a silent *h*: an ending, an eerie noise.
- Use **the** before words beginning with any letter: the site, the passengers.

An adjective formed from a proper noun is a **proper adjective**. Proper adjectives are capitalized: American newspapers.

**Directions** Underline the articles and circle the adjectives in each sentence.

1. An iceberg is a huge mass of ice that has broken off from a glacier.
2. A large iceberg can weigh a million tons and stretch many miles.
3. In the Atlantic Ocean, most icebergs come from the island of Greenland.
4. Icebergs are made of frozen fresh water.
5. For travelers, they are beautiful and deadly.
6. As they float south, icebergs melt in the warm sun.

**Directions** Write *a, an,* or *the* to complete each sentence. Use the article that makes sense.

7. Some icebergs are carried by wind into ______ Atlantic Ocean.
8. Only ______ small part of an iceberg is visible above the water.
9. ______ iceberg is quite impressive to behold.

**Directions** Complete each sentence with an adjective or adjectives of your own.

10. The wreck of the ____________ ship lies in ____________ pieces on the ocean floor.
11. A litter of belongings tells the ____________ tale of lost life.
12. The once ____________ ship is now a ____________ heap on the ocean floor.

**Home Activity** Your child learned about adjectives and articles. Ask your child to expand sentences such as the following by adding adjectives and articles: *The ship sank. It struck an iceberg. People died. Today it's a legend.*

Name ______________________________

# Adjectives and Articles

**Directions** Choose an adjective from the box to complete each sentence.

| hollow | Greek | strange | deep-sea |
|---|---|---|---|
| several | five | 4,500 | |

**1.** *Bathys* is a ______________ word meaning "deep," and a *sphere* is a globe or ball.

**2.** The bathysphere was the first ______________ machine that took people far beneath the waves.

**3.** This ______________ steel ball, which weighed ______________ pounds, was raised and lowered by a cable.

**4.** It was about ______________ feet in diameter and was fitted inside with oxygen tanks.

**5.** Divers reported news of the ______________ animals they saw via a telephone cable to a ship on the surface.

**6.** ______________ creatures had never been seen by humans before!

**Directions** Think about what you would like to see on a visit to the ocean floor. Write a sentence to answer each question below. Use adjectives and articles and underline them.

**7.** How far down would you travel?

______________________________________________

______________________________________________

**8.** What equipment would you take?

______________________________________________

______________________________________________

**9.** What would you look for?

______________________________________________

______________________________________________

**10.** What do you think it would look like?

______________________________________________

______________________________________________

**Home Activity** Your child learned how to write adjectives and articles correctly. Ask your child to write a paragraph describing what it is like to move under water. Have him or her circle adjectives and articles used.

Name ______________________

# Adjectives and Articles

**Directions** Mark the letter of the adjective in each sentence.

**1.** *Alvin* is a small American submarine used to explore the ocean.
**A** Alvin
**B** American
**C** submarine
**D** ocean

**2.** Go for an eight-hour dive in *Alvin*.
**A** Go
**B** for
**C** eight-hour
**D** dive

**3.** Three people can fit inside.
**A** Three
**B** people
**C** fit
**D** inside

**4.** You can travel up to 4,500 meters below the surface.
**A** travel
**B** up
**C** 4,500
**D** below

**5.** On the bottom, you can conduct scientific experiments.
**A** bottom
**B** you
**C** conduct
**D** scientific

**6.** In the basket on the front of *Alvin*, you can load many instruments.
**A** basket
**B** front
**C** load
**D** many

**7.** Robotic arms help you move the equipment.
**A** Robotic
**B** help
**C** move
**D** equipment

**8.** *Alvin* carries lights to the dark ocean floor.
**A** lights
**B** to
**C** dark
**D** floor

**9.** *Alvin* has traveled to the bottom 4,000 times!
**A** has
**B** traveled
**C** bottom
**D** 4,000

**10.** The discovery of the *Titanic* was a famous adventure.
**A** discovery
**B** *Titanic*
**C** famous
**D** adventure

**Home Activity** Your child prepared for taking tests on adjectives and articles. Copy a page from a storybook. Have your child highlight the adjectives in red and the articles in blue.

Name ____________________________________________

# Adjectives and Articles

**Directions** Underline the articles and circle the adjectives in each sentence.

1. Huge icebergs break off the vast ice near Greenland.
2. One iceberg can be a dangerous object for ships at sea.
3. They look like beautiful islands, but they hide treacherous ice beneath the surface.
4. Most pilots keep a sharp lookout for icebergs.

**Directions** Write *what kind, how many,* or *which one* to tell what question each underlined adjective answers about a noun.

5. Many people enjoy going on cruises. ____________________
6. In 1912, trans-Atlantic travel required a ship. ____________________
7. Cruising was not the main reason for getting on board. ____________________
8. Those passengers were entertained royally. ____________________
9. There was plenty of rich food and drink. ____________________

**Directions** Write *a, an,* or *the* in the blank to complete each sentence. Choose the article that makes sense and follows the rules for articles.

10. They dressed for dinner almost ________ hour before it was served.
11. Mrs. Astor was escorted to her table by ________ captain.
12. ________ elegant glass dome rose over the grand staircase.
13. Fine linen, china, and silver gleamed upon ________ tables.
14. This glamour would all be gone in ________ few short hours.
15. But for now, the room was ________ magical place.
16. It was ________ most special spot in the world.

**Home Activity** Your child reviewed adjectives and articles. With your child, read an encyclopedia article about the *Titanic*. Ask your child to point out adjectives and articles in at least one paragraph.

Name ______________________________



# *This, That, These,* and *Those*

The adjectives *this, that, these,* and *those* tell which one or which ones. *This* and *that* modify singular nouns. *These* and *those* modify plural nouns. *This* and *these* refer to objects that are close by. *That* and *those* refer to objects farther away.

This shirt I have on is like that one in the store window.
These pencils just fit in the pocket, but those pens on the desk did not fit.

- Do not use *here* or *there* after *this, that, these,* or *those.*
  **No:** This here article is about NASA. That there one is about new computers.
  **Yes:** This article is about NASA. That one is about new computers.
- Do not use *them* in place of *these* or *those.*
  **No:** She wrote them articles for *Newsweek.*
  **Yes:** She wrote those articles for *Newsweek.*

**Directions** Write the letter of the sentence in which the underlined part is correct.

_____ **1. A** That there space capsule is smaller than I realized.
**B** That space capsule is smaller than I realized.

_____ **2. A** I think them astronauts were brave to travel in it.
**B** I think those astronauts were brave to travel in it.

_____ **3. A** Is that spacesuit the one worn by John Glenn?
**B** Is those spacesuit the one worn by John Glenn?

_____ **4. A** This here time line shows the history of space flight.
**B** This time line shows the history of space flight.

_____ **5. A** Robert Goddard helped design these early rockets.
**B** Robert Goddard helped design them early rockets.

**Directions** Write each sentence. Use the correct adjective in ( ).

**6.** Will (that, those) storm reach Florida today?

______________________________

**7.** If it does, NASA will postpone (this, these) shuttle launch.

______________________________

**8.** Use (them, those) binoculars to view the launch.

______________________________

School-Home CONNECTION **Home Activity** Your child learned about *this, that, these,* and *those*. Write the words on four index cards. Ask your child to match each word with the appropriate category: singular near, singular far, plural near, plural far.

Name ______________________

# *This, That, These, and Those*

**Directions** Think of an exciting new product that might come from the space program. Complete the following ad for this product. Use the adjectives *this, that*, *these,* or *those* and underline them.

These ______________________ are what America has been waiting for!

______________________________________________

______________________________________________

______________________________________________

______________________________________________

______________________________________________

______________________________________________

______________________ This ad has been brought to you by

______________________________________________

**Directions** Think about an object that you treasure. Tell what makes it special. Use the adjectives *this*, *that*, *these*, and *those* correctly.

______________________________________________

______________________________________________

______________________________________________

______________________________________________

______________________________________________

______________________________________________

______________________________________________

______________________________________________

______________________________________________

______________________________________________

______________________________________________

______________________________________________

**Home Activity** Your child learned how to use *this, that, these,* and *those* in writing. Ask your child to write sentences about things near and far, using each of the four adjectives correctly.

Name ______________________________



# *This, That, These, and Those*

**Directions** Mark the letter of the adjective that completes each sentence correctly.

**1.** ____ orange I'm eating is delicious.
- **A** This
- **B** That
- **C** These
- **D** Those

**2.** It is better than ____ apples from last week.
- **A** this
- **B** that
- **C** these
- **D** those

**3.** Astronauts don't get fresh fruit like ____ peaches we are eating.
- **A** this
- **B** that
- **C** these
- **D** those

**4.** ____ meals they take into space are freeze-dried.
- **A** This
- **B** That
- **C** These
- **D** Those

**5.** ____ fact means they must add water to them.
- **A** This here
- **B** That
- **C** These
- **D** Those there

**6.** Let's exchange ____ bread for these crackers.
- **A** this
- **B** that
- **C** these
- **D** those

**7.** Let's try some of ____ freeze-dried steak.
- **A** this here
- **B** them
- **C** those there
- **D** this

**8.** Is ____ water boiling yet?
- **A** this here
- **B** that
- **C** these here
- **D** that there

**9.** ____ granola bars are tasty too.
- **A** Them
- **B** This here
- **C** These here
- **D** These

**10.** Don't sign me up for ____ next shuttle flight.
- **A** that there
- **B** that
- **C** these here
- **D** these

**Home Activity** Your child prepared for taking tests on *this, that, these,* and *those*. Ask your child to use these adjectives with the names of objects you point out in a room to describe their number and location.

Name ______________________________

# This, That, These, and Those

**Directions** Match each adjective with the phrase that describes it.

_____ **1.** this — **A** modifies plural nouns that are close by

_____ **2.** that — **B** modifies singular nouns that are close by

_____ **3.** these — **C** modifies singular nouns that are far away

_____ **4.** those — **D** modifies plural nouns that are far away

**Directions** Underline the word in ( ) that completes each sentence correctly.

**5.** (This, Those) summer I am going to space camp.

**6.** At (that, these) camp we will train like astronauts.

**7.** Astronauts must take many tests, and one of (them, those) tests involves gravity.

**8.** Gravity pulls us to Earth. (This, These) force becomes very great when we try to leave Earth's atmosphere.

**9.** Takeoff pushes the spacecraft into space. During (this, those) minutes, the body has to withstand strong G-forces.

**10.** In space the body floats because it is weightless. I want to imitate (this, these) experience at camp.

**Directions** Write the sentences correctly.

**11.** Ellen Ochoa invented an optical system. That there system "sees" flaws in a repeating pattern.

______________________________

______________________________

______________________________

**12.** Ochoa holds three patents for inventions. Them inventions all involve optical systems or robotics.

______________________________

______________________________

______________________________

**Home Activity** Your child reviewed *this, that, these,* and *those.* Have your child read an encyclopedia or Internet biography about Ellen Ochoa and then summarize it using *this, that, these,* and *those.*

Name ______________________________

# Comparative and Superlative Adjectives

**Comparative adjectives** are used to compare two people, places, things, or groups. Add *-er* to most short adjectives to make their comparative forms. Use *more* with longer adjectives. **Superlative adjectives** are used to compare three or more people, places, things, or groups. Add *-est* to most short adjectives to make their superlative forms. Use *most* with longer adjectives.

| Adjective | Comparative | Superlative |
|---|---|---|
| great | greater | greatest |
| enormous | more enormous | most enormous |

- Adjectives such as *good* and *bad* have irregular comparative and superlative forms: *good, better, best; bad, worse, worst.*
- Never use *more* or *most* with *-er* and *-est.*
  *No:* more sillier, most ancientest
  *Yes:* sillier, most ancient

**Directions** Complete the table. Add *-er*, *-est*, *more*, or *most* as needed.

| Adjective | Comparative | Superlative |
|---|---|---|
| primitive | **1.** ______________ | **2.** ______________ |
| great | **3.** ______________ | **4.** ______________ |
| calm | **5.** ______________ | **6.** ______________ |
| wet | **7.** ______________ | **8.** ______________ |
| frightening | **9.** ______________ | **10.** ______________ |
| exciting | **11.** ______________ | **12.** ______________ |

**Directions** Write the correct forms of the adjectives in ( ) to complete the sentences.

**13.** Is Ray Bradbury ______________ (famous) than Jules Verne was?

**14.** Readers might think Jules Verne was the ______________ (lucky) science fiction writer of all.

**15.** Did Verne write ______________ (good) fiction than Lewis Carroll?

**16.** His ______________ (important) legacy of all was his influence on twentieth-century scientists, inventors, and explorers.

**Home Activity** Your child learned about comparative and superlative adjectives. Ask your child to use these forms to expand these sentences: *Science fiction is fascinating. Reading is fun. ____ is a good book.*

Name ___________________________

# Comparative and Superlative Adjectives

**Directions** Write a comparative or superlative form of the adjective in ( ) to make each sentence precise.

**1.** I think Jules Verne was a ______________ writer than Philip K. Dick. (inventive)

**2.** From childhood, he had been ______________ of all when observing how things worked. (happy)

**3.** He always researched the very ______________ scientific ideas. (new)

**4.** I like his books ______________ than those of Charles Dickens. (good)

**5.** Verne included the ______________ details possible in his novels. (realistic)

**6.** The submarine, motorcar, and navigable airship are just three inventions he anticipated from a ______________ age. (late)

**Directions** Write a paragraph to persuade a classmate to read one of your favorite books. Include comparative and superlative adjectives.

_______________________________________________

_______________________________________________

_______________________________________________

_______________________________________________

_______________________________________________

_______________________________________________

_______________________________________________

_______________________________________________

_______________________________________________

_______________________________________________

_______________________________________________

_______________________________________________

**Home Activity** Your child learned how to use comparative and superlative adjectives in writing. Ask your child to compare two of his or her favorite book characters using comparative and superlative adjectives.

Name ______________________________

# Comparative and Superlative Adjectives

**Directions** Mark the letter of the adjective form that correctly completes each sentence.

**1.** Most dinosaurs were ____ than today's reptiles.
**A** most big
**B** bigger
**C** biggest
**D** more big

**2.** *Tyrannosaurus rex* was the ____ dinosaur of all.
**A** scary
**B** more scary
**C** scarier
**D** scariest

**3.** Today, scientists have a ____ idea of what dinosaurs looked like than they used to.
**A** good
**B** best
**C** better
**D** more better

**4.** Sue is the ____ *T. rex* yet discovered.
**A** more large
**B** most large
**C** larger
**D** largest

**5.** She stands in one of the country's ____ natural history museums.
**A** finest
**B** most finest
**C** finer
**D** more finer

**6.** The Field Museum has the ____ dinosaur collection I have ever seen.
**A** bestest
**B** best
**C** good
**D** most best

**7.** The museum has many dinosaurs that are ____ than *T. rex*.
**A** smaller
**B** smallest
**C** more small
**D** most small

**8.** To many kids, dinosaurs are the ____ creatures in the world.
**A** fascinatingest
**B** fascinatinger
**C** most fascinating
**D** more fascinating

**9.** Dinosaurs appear ____ in science fiction than in romance novels.
**A** more often
**B** most often
**C** more oftener
**D** most oftenest

**10.** Which of these two books do you think is ____?
**A** excitingest
**B** excitinger
**C** most exciting
**D** more exciting

**Home Activity** Your child prepared for taking tests on comparative and superlative adjectives. Ask your child to use the correct adjective forms on this page in sentences to compare sets of two objects, then sets of three objects.

Name ______________________________

# Comparative and Superlative Adjectives

**Directions** If the adjective forms are correct, write *Correct* on the line. If they are not correct, write the comparative and superlative forms correctly on the line.

| | Adjective | Comparative | Superlative | |
|---|---|---|---|---|
| **1.** | happy | more happier | most happiest | ______________________ |
| **2.** | hungry | hungrier | hungriest | ______________________ |
| **3.** | beloved | beloveder | belovedest | ______________________ |
| **4.** | sad | more sadder | most saddest | ______________________ |

**Directions** Underline the adjective form in ( ) to complete each sentence correctly.

**5.** Jules Verne was (most unhappy, most unhappiest) as a stockbroker.

**6.** He was (happier, more happier) writing plays.

**7.** However, he was a much (more better, better) novelist than a playwright.

**8.** He left business and went on to become the (more successful, most successful) writer of his time.

**9.** He wrote more books than other authors, and they were of (higher, most highest) quality.

**10.** They were scientifically accurate, but readers found them (entertaininger, more entertaining) than educational.

**Directions** Write the correct forms of the adjectives in ( ) to complete the sentences.

**11.** The Earth has three layers. Which layer is ____________________? (thin)

**12.** The outer layer, called the crust, is the ____________________ layer of the three. (rigid)

**13.** The middle layer, called the mantle, contains melted rock and is much ____________________ than the crust. (hot)

**14.** The core, in the Earth's center, is under the ____________________ pressure of all. (intense)

**15.** Jules Verne's idea for a journey to the core is ____________________ than realistic. (fantastic)

**Home Activity** Your child reviewed comparative and superlative adjectives. Reread the selection with your child. Have him or her describe the fighting monsters using comparative and superlative adjectives.

Name ____________________________

# Adverbs

**Adverbs** tell more about verbs. They explain *how, when,* or *where* actions happen. Many adverbs that tell *how* end in *-ly*. Adverbs can appear before or after the verbs they describe.

| | |
|---|---|
| **How** | Cowboys rode expertly. They worked hard. |
| **When** | They seldom slept past daybreak. They always took care of their horses. |
| **Where** | A cowtown existed here. Cowboys visited there for entertainment. |

Some adverbs tell more about an adjective or another adverb:

A ghost town seems rather spooky to me. I very rarely go to such places.

**Comparative adverbs** compare two actions. Add *-er* to form a comparative adverb. **Superlative adverbs** compare three or more actions. Add *-est* to form a superlative adverb. If an adverb ends in *-ly*, use *more* or *most* instead of *-er* or *-est*.

| | |
|---|---|
| **Comparative Adverb** | The stagecoach rolled more slowly going up the mountain than going down. |
| **Superlative Adverb** | When they were fresh, the horses pulled most quickly of all. |

- The adverbs *well* and *badly* use special forms to show comparison.

| Adverb | Comparative | Superlative |
|---|---|---|
| well | better | best |
| badly | worse | worst |

**Directions** Underline the adverb or adverbs in each sentence. Circle the word that each adverb tells more about.

1. Pioneer women bravely risked their lives.
2. They worked tirelessly to feed and clothe their families.
3. They seldom shopped at a store.
4. They were often lonely in their isolated homes.
5. They toiled outdoors in gardens and indoors at wood stoves.

**Directions** Underline the correct adverb in ( ) to complete each sentence.

6. We can point (proudly, more proudly) at the staying power of pioneers.
7. They lived with hardship (better, more better) than I would have.
8. If crops failed, they faced a (terrible, terribly) hard winter.
9. Towns needed railroads (more desperately, most desperately) than they needed settlers.
10. Railroads connected settlers (direct, directly) to supplies and goods.

**Home Activity** Your child learned about adverbs. Ask your child to expand these sentences using adverbs to tell how, when, and where: *Settlers traveled. They built homes and towns. They raised food.*

Name ______________________________

# Adverbs

**Directions** Write an adverb on the line to make each sentence more lively and colorful.

**1.** The prospector whispered ______________________, "Can it be?"

**2.** Then he began to leap and dance ______________________ around the campsite.

**3.** The large lump in the pan gleamed ______________________ in the sunlight.

**4.** The assayer's report erased his joy ______________________.

**5.** The old man limped ______________________ back to camp.

**6.** He said ______________________, "It was only fool's gold."

**Directions** Imagine you are touring a ghost town in the Old West. Write a paragraph describing how the town looks and what is happening there. Use adverbs to help make your description vivid and colorful.

______________________________________________________________________

______________________________________________________________________

______________________________________________________________________

______________________________________________________________________

______________________________________________________________________

______________________________________________________________________

______________________________________________________________________

______________________________________________________________________

______________________________________________________________________

______________________________________________________________________

______________________________________________________________________

______________________________________________________________________

______________________________________________________________________

**Home Activity** Your child learned how to use adverbs in writing. With your child, make up a story about a cowboy's trip to town. Encourage your child to include adverbs to make actions vivid and precise.

Name ______________________________

# Adverbs

**Directions** Mark the letter of the word that is an adverb in each sentence.

**1.** Pete sometimes pretends he is a strong, silent cowboy.
**A** sometimes
**B** pretends
**C** strong
**D** silent

**2.** He practices lassoing fenceposts faithfully.
**A** he
**B** lassoing
**C** fenceposts
**D** faithfully

**3.** He wears a very old ten-gallon hat.
**A** ten-gallon
**B** a
**C** very
**D** hat

**4.** Pete is anxiously waiting for his birthday.
**A** Pete
**B** anxiously
**C** waiting
**D** his

**5.** He has always dreamed of having a horse.
**A** always
**B** dreamed
**C** having
**D** horse

**Directions** Write the letter of the correct answer to each question.

**6.** Which word or phrase is the comparative form of the adverb *quickly*?
**A** quicklier
**B** quickliest
**C** more quickly
**D** most quickly

**7.** Which word or phrase is the superlative form of the adverb *badly*?
**A** worse
**B** worst
**C** more badly
**D** most badly

**8.** Which word is an adverb that tells when an action occurred?
**A** downtown
**B** slowly
**C** easily
**D** never

**Home Activity** Your child prepared for taking tests on adverbs. Have your child read a favorite story aloud, point out the adverbs, and tell what words they describe. Encourage your child to add adverbs to the story.

Name ______________________________

# Adverbs

**Directions** Write the comparative and superlative forms of each adverb.

| Adverb | Comparative Adverb | Superlative Adverb |
|---|---|---|
| fast | 1. ____________ | 2. ____________ |
| hard | 3. ____________ | 4. ____________ |
| eagerly | 5. ____________ | 6. ____________ |
| badly | 7. ____________ | 8. ____________ |

**Directions** Underline the adverb in each sentence. Circle the word or words that each adverb tells more about.

5. The man looked extremely nervous.
6. He waited impatiently for the stage.
7. It seemed as though it would never arrive.
8. Finally, he heard a storm of hooves.
9. The dusty stage rolled westward toward town.
10. The man greeted his bride warmly.

**Directions** Underline the correct adverb in ( ) to complete each sentence.

11. California was settled (sooner, more sooner) than many Western states.
12. The promise of gold (first, firstly) drew miners and settlers.
13. Good climate and fertile land held them there (more successfully, most successfully) though.
14. Nevada treated its settlers (harshlier, more harshly) than California.
15. When the silver ran out, miners (quickly, most quickly) left Nevada's hot, dry territory.

**Home Activity** Your child reviewed adverbs. Have your child clip adjectives from magazine advertisements, change them into adverbs, write the comparative and superlative form of each adverb, and use both forms in sentences.

Name ______________________________

# Modifiers

Adjectives, adverbs, and prepositional phrases are **modifiers**, words or groups of words that tell more about, or modify, other words in a sentence. Adjectives modify nouns and pronouns. Adverbs modify verbs, adjectives, or other adverbs. Prepositional phrases can act as adjectives or adverbs.

**As Adjective** The sand at the beach felt hard and smooth.
**As Adverb** Waves crashed on the sand.

- To avoid confusion, place modifiers close to the words they modify. Adjective phrases usually come right after the word they modify. Adverb phrases may appear right after a verb or at the beginning of a sentence.
- The meaning of a sentence can be unclear if the modifier is misplaced.

  *No:* Green umbrellas from the sun shaded people.
  *Yes:* Green umbrellas shaded people from the sun.
- The position of *only* in a sentence can affect the sentence's entire meaning. Place *only* directly before the word or words it modifies.

  *Example:* Only she ate eggs. (Nobody else ate them.)
  She only ate eggs. (She didn't do anything except eat.)
  She ate only eggs. (She ate nothing else.)

**Directions** Write *adverb, adjective,* or *prepositional phrase* to identify each underlined modifier. Write *adjective* or *adverb* to identify how a prepositional phrase is used.

1. The Papadopolous family lives near the beach. ______________________________
2. Their large tribe of children loves beachcombing. ______________________________
3. They can be found outside on the beach each morning. ______________________________

**Directions** Each sentence has a misplaced modifier. Rewrite the sentence and put the phrase where it belongs.

4. We rented a boat from a man with an outboard motor.

______________________________

______________________________

5. Bonnie picked up a pretty seashell with a cheerful grin.

______________________________

______________________________

**Home Activity** Your child learned about modifiers. With your child, read a newspaper article. Ask your child to identify several modifiers, including adjectives, adverbs, and prepositional phrases.

Name ______________________

# Modifiers

**Directions** Add adjectives, adverbs, and prepositional phrases to these sentences. Use modifiers to create a more specific, interesting picture.

**1.** A dog barked and ran.

______________________

______________________

**2.** The sun set.

______________________

______________________

**3.** Families packed their gear and left.

______________________

______________________

**4.** Waves washed and crabs scurried.

______________________

______________________

**Directions** Imagine you are at a beach and you find something exciting or interesting. Write a description of what you find and how you find it. Use modifiers to create a vivid word picture.

______________________

______________________

______________________

______________________

______________________

______________________

______________________

______________________

**Home Activity** Your child learned how to use modifiers in writing. Give your child simple sentences like those in items 1–4 on this page and have him or her add modifiers to make interesting story starters.

Name ______________________________



# Modifiers

**Directions** Mark the letter of the item that correctly identifies the underlined word or words in each sentence.

**1.** Taryanna collected pink seashells.

**A** adjective
**B** adverb
**C** prepositional phrase/adjective
**D** prepositional phrase/adverb

**2.** Marcus built a sand castle with a moat.

**A** adjective
**B** adverb
**C** prepositional phrase/adjective
**D** prepositional phrase/adverb

**3.** The sun shone brightly.

**A** adjective
**B** adverb
**C** prepositional phrase/adjective
**D** prepositional phrase/adverb

**4.** Some wild horses galloped in the wet sand.

**A** adjective
**B** adverb
**C** prepositional phrase/adjective
**D** prepositional phrase/adverb

**5.** Everyone chattered and pointed at the horses.

**A** adjective
**B** adverb
**C** prepositional phrase/adjective
**D** prepositional phrase/adverb

**6.** A small herd has roamed the beach for years.

**A** adjective
**B** adverb
**C** prepositional phrase/adjective
**D** prepositional phrase/adverb

**Directions** Mark the letter of the sentence that has a misplaced modifier.

**7.** **A** The fresh popcorn smelled wonderful.
**B** There was a long line at the concession stand.
**C** Several hungry children waited impatiently.
**D** Vendors sold ice cream treats in white hats.

**8.** **A** They decorated the sand castle with sea shells.
**B** It had four towers and a red flag.
**C** A boy tossed a ball in a red shirt.
**D** Only Jill wanted to knock down the castle.

**Home Activity** Your child prepared for taking tests on modifiers. Copy a paragraph from one of your child's favorite stories, leaving blanks where modifiers go. Ask your child to suggest possible modifiers for the blanks. Compare with the original.

Name ______________________________



# Modifiers

**Directions** Underline the prepositional phrase in each sentence. Write *adverb* or *adjective* to identify how the prepositional phrase is used.

**1.** Do you like swimming in the ocean? ____________________

**2.** The water around my feet is inviting and cool. ____________________

**3.** Jorge rides the waves on his surfboard. ____________________

**4.** See the beach ball by the umbrella. ____________________

**5.** You float easily in sea water. ____________________

**6.** The huge sea turtle with the green shell blinked sleepily. ____________________

**Directions** Underline the adjectives, adverbs, and prepositional phrases in each sentence. The number in ( ) tells how many modifiers a sentence contains. (Do not underline the articles *a* and *the*.)

**7.** The two families shared a delicious picnic under the trees. (3)

**8.** Spicy Cuban food cooked slowly on the grill. (4)

**9.** Mom made crispy tortillas in a skillet. (2)

**10.** Thirsty children drank cold lemonade in the shade. (3)

**11.** A busy army of ants marched into the salad. (3)

**Directions** Underline the misplaced modifier in each sentence. Rewrite the sentence, and put the modifier where it belongs.

**12.** Ona only photographed the seagulls—nothing else.

____________________________________________

____________________________________________

**13.** Lee could see a pelican dive through his binoculars.

____________________________________________

____________________________________________

**14.** The man signaled to me with a moustache.

____________________________________________

____________________________________________

**Home Activity** Your child reviewed modifiers. Have your child use a magazine article or story to show you good examples of adjectives, adverbs, and prepositional phrases that make the writing specific and interesting.

Name ______________________________

# Conjunctions

A conjunction is a word such as *and, but,* or *or* that joins words, phrases, and sentences.

- Use *and* to join related ideas: The snowy owl and snow bunting are arctic birds.
- Use *but* to join contrasting ideas: I like the snow but not the cold.
- Use *or* to suggest a choice: Is that a ringed seal or a hooded seal?

You can use conjunctions to make compound subjects, compound predicates, and compound sentences. Place a comma before the conjunction in a compound sentence.

| | |
|---|---|
| **Compound Subject** | Frigid cold and deep snow make arctic life difficult. |
| **Compound Predicate** | Arctic foxes do not hibernate but withstand the cold. |
| **Compound Sentence** | They feed on live prey, or they can eat remains of a polar bear's meal. |

**Directions** Underline the conjunction(s) in each sentence.

**1.** The arctic fox makes a burrow in a hill or cliff, but it does not hibernate.

**2.** It is well adapted for the cold with its furry feet and small, rounded ears.

**3.** A polar bear is huge but surprisingly fast and can outrun a caribou.

**Directions** Underline the conjunction in ( ) that completes each sentence.

**4.** The tundra has very little moisture (or, and) a short growing season.

**5.** The climate is harsh, (or, but) more than 1,700 kinds of plants live in the Arctic.

**Directions** Use the conjunction *and, but,* or *or* to join each pair of sentences. Write the new sentences. Remember to add a comma.

**6.** The Arctic is frigid in winter. It is much warmer in summer.

______________________________________________

______________________________________________

**7.** Arctic plants must grow quickly. They won't have time to reproduce.

______________________________________________

______________________________________________

**Home Activity** Your child learned about conjunctions. Have your child write *and, but,* and *or* on index cards and then read a short article, making a tally mark on the appropriate card each time he or she sees that conjunction.

Name ______________________________

# Conjunctions

**Directions** Write a conjunction on each line to complete the paragraph.

**(1)** The island features spectacular cliffs ______________ volcanic mountains. **(2)** That odd seabird you observed might be a petrel ______________ a fulmar. **(3)** The climate is extremely cold, ______________ many birds are able to live here. **(4)** They build their nests in the cliffs ______________ raise their young. **(5)** Birds can breed on the island, ______________ they need not stay all year. **(6)** Some birds migrate to warmer winter headquarters, ______________ others build up an insulating layer of fat. **(7)** One bird you are sure to see is McKay's bunting, which breeds here ______________ nowhere else.

**Directions** Combine the short sentences to make one longer, smoother sentence. Use conjunctions. Write the new sentence.

**8.** In 1944, voles lived on St. Matthew Island. So did arctic foxes.

______________________________________________

______________________________________________

______________________________________________

______________________________________________

**9.** The Coast Guard introduced 24 female reindeer to the island. They also introduced 5 males.

______________________________________________

______________________________________________

______________________________________________

______________________________________________

**10.** Years before there were reindeer everywhere. Now only a few remained.

______________________________________________

______________________________________________

______________________________________________

______________________________________________

**Home Activity** Your child learned how to use conjunctions in writing. Have your child read about reindeer and write simple sentences about them. Ask your child to find ways to combine some of the related sentences.

Name ______________________________

# Conjunctions

**Directions** Mark the letter of the word that best completes each sentence.

**1.** Which is bigger: a reindeer ____ an elk?
**A** however
**B** also
**C** but
**D** or

**2.** Reptiles ____ amphibians do not live in the Arctic.
**A** and
**B** if
**C** because
**D** but

**3.** It is too cold ____ dry for them there.
**A** but
**B** and
**C** or
**D** however

**4.** Female reindeer do have antlers, ____ males have much larger ones.
**A** anyway
**B** if
**C** but
**D** or

**5.** Did the reindeer die of disease ____ hunger?
**A** because
**B** also
**C** but
**D** or

**6.** Some of the deer survived, ____ most of them starved.
**A** but
**B** or
**C** and
**D** because

**7.** Forty-one females ____ one male were alive.
**A** so
**B** and
**C** but
**D** when

**8.** They did not produce young, ____ the herd soon died out.
**A** and
**B** or
**C** until
**D** but

**9.** This is an unfortunate ____ predictable story.
**A** for
**B** or
**C** but
**D** because

**10.** The island had too little space ____ not enough predators.
**A** until
**B** and
**C** when
**D** but

**Home Activity** Your child prepared for taking tests on conjunctions. Have your child find and circle *and, but,* and *or* in ads. Ask your child to explain why each word is used.

Name ______________________________

# Conjunctions

**Directions** Underline the conjunction in each sentence.

**1.** Birds and small mammals live on the island.

**2.** Did a fox or a rabbit make that nest?

**3.** Count the animals on the island, and we will make a chart.

**4.** You can count them but cannot determine their sex.

**5.** We will find out what happened or guess the cause of the die-off.

**Directions** Underline the conjunction in ( ) that completes each sentence.

**6.** Nature holds many mysteries, (and, or) scientists want to solve them.

**7.** Scientists use logic and scientific method, (or, but) imagination is also important.

**8.** Dr. David Klein had to count (and, or) also weigh reindeer on St. Matthew Island.

**9.** He knew the reindeer were not killed by diseases (but, or) parasites.

**10.** Low weight (or, and) missing bone marrow suggested the deer had starved.

**Directions** Use the conjunction *and, but,* or *or* to join each pair of sentences. Write the new sentences. Remember to add a comma.

**11.** Polar mammals have fur and fat to keep them warm. People have to dress warmly.

______________________________

______________________________

______________________________

______________________________

**12.** Layers of clothing trap warm air next to the skin. This keeps people warm in cold weather.

______________________________

______________________________

______________________________

______________________________

**Home Activity** Your child reviewed conjunctions. With your child, make a favorite food. Ask your child to talk about the process, using the conjunctions *and, but,* and *or* to describe actions and choices in the process.

Name ______________________________



# Commas

**Commas** can clarify meaning and tell readers when to pause.

- Put a comma after every item in a *series* but the last.
  Poets pay attention to the sounds**,** meanings**,** and emotions of words.
  The audience applauded**,** cheered**,** and stood up.
- When you speak or write to someone, you may use the person's name or title. This noun of *direct address* is set off with a comma, or two commas if it is in the middle of a sentence.
  Will you read some more**,** Mr. Berry?
  I'd love to**,** children**,** if you aren't tired of sitting.
- *Appositives* are noun phrases that describe another noun. They are set off by commas.
  Ted Kooser**,** a wonderful poet**,** lives in Nebraska.
- Put a comma after an *introductory word or phrase,* such as *yes, no, well, of course,* or *in fact.*
  No**,** I haven't read the new book. As usual**,** I'm too busy.

**Directions** Add commas to each sentence where they are needed.

1. Harry enjoys writing stories poems and articles.
2. Voni do you prefer reading fairy tales tall tales or myths?
3. *King Midas* a myth about values features a greedy king.
4. Were you surprised Kaela when the glowing young man appeared?
5. No I expect magical things to happen in tales.
6. King Midas's gift is deadly because he cannot eat drink or touch people.

**Directions** Rewrite each sentence. Add commas where they are needed.

7. By the way King Midas what did you learn about gold?

______________________________

______________________________

8. I learned that gold is cold hard and meaningless by itself.

______________________________

______________________________

**Home Activity** Your child learned about commas. Record a short conversation with your child about his or her favorite foods or activities. Ask your child to write the conversation adding commas where they are needed.

Name ______________________________

# Commas

**Directions** Add commas in the sentences to make the meaning clear. Rewrite the paragraph.

**(1)** Some things are necessities items we could not live without. **(2)** Food water and shelter fit in this category. **(3)** What more do we need dear reader to live and be happy? **(4)** Many people believe they would be happy if only they had lots of money possessions and free time. **(5)** In fact people's real needs are quite different. **(6)** The happiest people are those who have good health loving relationships and useful work.

______________________________
______________________________
______________________________
______________________________
______________________________
______________________________
______________________________
______________________________
______________________________
______________________________

**Directions** Write sentences to answer each question. Use commas to set off words in a series, appositives, words of direct address, and introductory words.

**7.** What are three possessions that are precious to you?

______________________________
______________________________
______________________________

**8.** Explain why one of these objects is important to you. Address your sentences to a friend.

______________________________
______________________________
______________________________

**Home Activity** Your child learned how to use commas in writing. With your child, read a story or article. Have your child point out commas that are used to set off series, appositives, introductory words, and nouns of direct address.

Name ______________________________

# Commas

**Directions** Mark the letter of the choice that tells why commas are used in each sentence.

**1.** The king ate porridge, toast, and jam.
**A** series
**B** appositive
**C** introductory word
**D** direct address

**2.** Dad, do you know this story?
**A** series
**B** appositive
**C** introductory word
**D** direct address

**3.** This story is a myth, a kind of story.
**A** series
**B** appositive
**C** introductory word
**D** direct address

**4.** Yes, it has a happy ending.
**A** series
**B** appositive
**C** introductory word
**D** direct address

**Directions** Mark the letter of the choice that shows the word or words and punctuation needed to complete each sentence correctly.

**5.** A king's castle had a drawbridge, ____ lookout towers.
**A** a moat and
**B** a moat and,
**C** a moat, and
**D** a moat, and,

**6.** Look at this picture ____ Cate.
**A** of, a castle,
**B** of a castle,
**C** of a castle
**D** of a castle;

**7.** Medieval castles were ____ homes.
**A** fortresses gathering places and
**B** fortresses, gathering places and,
**C** fortresses, gathering places and
**D** fortresses, gathering places, and

**8.** ____ have you ever seen a castle?
**A** Henry,
**B** Henry
**C** Henry;
**D** , Henry

**9.** ____ castles sat on a hilltop and had high stone walls.
**A** Usually,
**B** Usually
**C** Usually;
**D** Usually.

**10.** Castles were designed as ____ attack.
**A** fortresses; strongholds against
**B** fortresses. Strongholds against
**C** fortresses, strongholds against
**D** fortresses strongholds against

**11.** A castle usually had a ____ around it.
**A** moat; a water-filled ditch;
**B** moat, a water-filled ditch,
**C** moat. A water-filled ditch
**D** moat a water -filled ditch

**12.** ____ a moat did not always have water in it.
**A** No,
**B** No;
**C** No
**D** No.

**Home Activity** Your child prepared for taking tests on commas. Ask your child to give example sentences to teach you about the four uses of commas he or she learned.

Name ______________________________

# Commas

**Directions** Add commas to each sentence where they are needed.

**1.** Many tales involve kingdoms magic creatures and wishes.

**2.** Have you noticed Danny that humans always seem to use these wishes foolishly?

**3.** Yes tales also often have a young person as the hero.

**4.** Tales usually have a talking animal stone or tree.

**5.** One tale featured Excalibur a sword with a mind of its own.

**6.** Mr. Wickness our reading teacher said we could write a tale a mystery or a poem.

**Directions** Rewrite each sentence. Add commas where they are needed.

**7.** Gold has been used for centuries to make coins jewelry and accessories.

______________________________

______________________________

**8.** Can you tell me Mr. Liakos if the king's crown is made of gold?

______________________________

______________________________

**9.** Yes it is made of gold and inset with precious gems.

______________________________

______________________________

**10.** Both crown and scepter a staff symbolizing the king's power were made of valuable materials.

______________________________

______________________________

**11.** In fact the scepter has more diamonds on it than the crown does.

______________________________

______________________________

**Home Activity** Your child reviewed commas. Ask your child to write an imaginary conversation between two friends about their favorite things. Have your child highlight the commas in another color.

Name ______________________________



# Quotations and Quotation Marks

A **direct quotation** gives a person's exact words and is enclosed in **quotation marks** (" "). Direct quotations begin with capital letters and end with proper punctuation. End punctuation is inside the closing quotation marks. Words that tell who is speaking are set off from the quotation by punctuation.

- When the quotation comes last in a sentence, set it off with a comma.
  Jamie asked, "What was the *Hindenburg?*"
- When the quotation comes first in a sentence, a comma, question mark, or exclamation mark sets off the quotation.
  "It was a dirigible," replied May. "It was enormous!" she added.
- When the quotation is interrupted by words that tell who is speaking, use two sets of quotation marks. Notice that words telling who is speaking are followed by punctuation. Use a comma if the second part of the quotation does not begin a new sentence.
  "Dirigibles were lighter than air," he added, "because they were filled with hydrogen."
- Use end punctuation and a capital letter if the second part of the quotation does begin a new sentence.
  "Isn't hydrogen flammable?" asked Jamie. "What kept it from exploding?"

**Directions** Rewrite each sentence. Add quotation marks where they are needed.

**1.** Are the blimps dirigibles? asked Max.

______________________________

**2.** No, they aren't, explained Vi, because they aren't rigid.

______________________________

______________________________

**Directions** Write each sentence correctly. Add capital letters, quotation marks, and other punctuation as needed.

**3.** Vi said the framework is like a skeleton

______________________________

**4.** fabric covers it she added like skin

______________________________

**Home Activity** Your child learned about quotations and quotation marks. With your child, find quotations in a newspaper or magazine article. Have your child highlight the quotation marks and other punctuation and explain why they are used.

Name ______________________________

# Quotations and Quotation Marks

**Directions** Choose a sentence from the box that supports the ideas in each paragraph. Write the sentence, adding quotation marks and correct punctuation.

> A radio announcer moaned over the airwaves Oh, the humanity!
>
> Modern airships are generally known only as flying billboards one expert says.
>
> As airship historian R. D. Layman explains A balloon cannot be piloted in any sense of the word.

1. The hot air balloon and airship differ in important ways. An airship is powered by a motor and propellers, but a balloon is not. An airship's horizontal path can be controlled, but a balloon's cannot. A balloon can be raised or lowered by adjusting the propane burner that heats the air inside it. However, it goes wherever the wind takes it.

   ______________________________________________

   ______________________________________________

2. The burning of the *Hindenburg* on May 6, 1937, is the most famous airship disaster. The spectacular accident was witnessed by many and actually covered on the air. It turned the public away from airships. They watched as the enormous fireball plummeted from the sky and people lost their lives. One cry in particular spoke for the American public.

   ______________________________________________

   ______________________________________________

**Directions** Do you think airship travel should have been abandoned or continued? On another sheet of paper, write a paragraph to persuade readers that your opinion is correct. Use quotations from *The Hindenburg* to support your argument. Use quotation marks and punctuation to set off your quotations correctly.

______________________________________________

______________________________________________

______________________________________________

______________________________________________

______________________________________________

______________________________________________

______________________________________________

**Home Activity** Your child learned how to use quotations and quotation marks in writing. With your child, write dialogue for characters in a story about flying. Have your child punctuate the dialogue correctly.

Name ______________________________



# Quotations and Quotation Marks

**Directions** Mark the letter of the item that completes each sentence correctly.

**1.** "I'm going on a hot-air balloon ____ said Sherry.
**A** ride"
**B** ride."
**C** ride,"
**D** ride?"

**2.** "Wow! That's so ____ exclaimed Phil.
**A** cool"
**B** cool!"
**C** cool."
**D** cool?"

**3.** He asked ____ you think I could come too?"
**A** earnestly, "Do
**B** earnestly "Do
**C** earnestly "do
**D** earnestly. "Do

**4.** "I'll ask my ____ Sherry said.
**A** dad."
**B** dad,"
**C** dad"
**D** dad?"

**5.** "What is it ____ inquired Phil.
**A** like,"
**B** like."
**C** like?,"
**D** like?"

**6.** She replied ____ like floating on a cloud."
**A** dreamily, "it's
**B** dreamily. "It's
**C** dreamily, "It's
**D** dreamily "It's

**7.** "The buildings and cars below look like ____ continued.
**A** toys," she
**B** toys," She
**C** toys" she
**D** toys." She

**8.** "How do you make it go up and ____ Phil.
**A** down? asked
**B** down," asked
**C** down?" asked
**D** down?" Asked

**9.** "A burner heats the ____ Sherry.
**A** air, explained
**B** air," Explained
**C** air" explained
**D** air," explained

**10.** "More hot air takes you ____ less takes you down."
**A** up," she said. "and"
**B** up," She said, "And
**C** up," she said, "and
**D** up." she said. "And

**Home Activity** Your child prepared for taking tests on quotations and quotation marks. Have your child interview you about your day and write your reply as a quotation, beginning with *He/She said* and using quotation marks correctly.

Name ______________________________

# Quotations and Quotation Marks

**Directions** Rewrite each sentence. Add quotation marks where they are needed.

**1.** Tell us about blimps, requested Sean.

______________________________

**2.** What do you want to know? asked the museum guide.

______________________________

______________________________

**3.** Sean asked Do they have a framework inside to give them shape?

______________________________

______________________________

**4.** They do not, replied the guide. They get their shape from the gas inside them.

______________________________

______________________________

**Directions** Write each sentence correctly. Add capital letters, quotation marks, and other punctuation as needed.

**5.** Blimps are filled with helium he continued

______________________________

**6.** how are they used asked Sean

______________________________

**7.** the military has used blimps he replied to learn where land mines are located

______________________________

______________________________

**8.** some companies use them for advertising he continued and for aerial views of sports events

______________________________

______________________________

______________________________

**Home Activity** Your child reviewed quotations and quotation marks. Ask your child to write sentences about the *Hindenburg* and include dialogue. Remind your child to use quotation marks and other punctuation correctly.

Name ______________________________

# Punctuation

You have already learned about punctuation such as commas, quotation marks, and end marks. Here are some other kinds of punctuation.

- A **colon (:)** is used to separate hours and minutes in expressions of time. It is also used after the salutation in a business letter.
  10:30 A.M.   9:15 P.M.   Dear Ms. Glover:   Sir:
- A **hyphen (-)** is used in some compound words. Two common uses are numbers from twenty-one to ninety-nine and compound words that are thought of as one word.
  old-time music   best-known book   forty-nine   five-year-old boy
- A **semicolon (;)** can be used to join two independent clauses instead of a comma and a conjunction.
  Jazz is a mixture of different types of music**;** New Orleans was its birthplace.
- **Italics** or **underlining** is used for titles of books, newspapers, magazines, and works of art. Because you cannot write italics, underline titles in your writing.
  the *Chicago Tribune* (newspaper)   *Time for Kids* (magazine)
  *or*   the Chicago Tribune   Time for Kids
- A **dash (—)** sets off information or a comment that interrupts the flow of a sentence.
  Jazz had developed many styles—bebop and Dixieland, for example—by the 1940s.

**Directions** Rewrite each sentence on the lines. Add punctuation where it is needed.

**1.** Jinny is writing a how to book titled You Can Do Most Anything.

______________________________

______________________________

**2.** The first show is at 800 P.M. the second is at 1030 P.M.

______________________________

______________________________

**3.** Cuthbert we call him Chip is my best friend.

______________________________

**4.** Mae made a last minute effort to learn twenty two songs.

______________________________

______________________________

**Home Activity** Your child learned about punctuation. Have your child explain and model a use for colons and semicolons.

Name ______________________________

# Punctuation

**Directions** Add the punctuation named in ( ) to make the meaning of the sentence clear. Write the sentence.

**1.** A clarinet is a woodwind instrument it makes sounds when air vibrates inside it. (semicolon)

______________________________

______________________________

**2.** Woodwinds were once made of wood now they are also made of other materials. (semicolon)

______________________________

______________________________

**3.** The after school program will show the movie Music Man at 300 P.M. (hyphen, underlining, colon)

______________________________

______________________________

**Directions** Add punctuation to the following paragraph to make it clear. Rewrite the paragraph.

The clarinet is a single reed woodwind instrument. Its thin, flat reed is attached to the mouthpiece. The clarinet player takes the mouthpiece in her mouth and blows then the reed vibrates against the mouthpiece. Vibrating air is pushed through the straight, tube shaped instrument. Fingers press keys to open and close holes. A good clarinet player that's not me yet can make a wide range of smooth sounds.

______________________________

______________________________

______________________________

______________________________

______________________________

______________________________

______________________________

______________________________

**Home Activity** Your child learned how to use punctuation in writing. With your child, write a letter to a music store asking about a special CD. Be sure your child includes appropriate punctuation marks.

Name ______________________________



# Punctuation

**Directions** Mark the name of the punctuation mark that matches the definition.

**1.** Used to join two independent clauses
- **A** colon
- **B** dash
- **C** semicolon
- **D** hyphen

**2.** Used to set off information that interrupts a sentence
- **A** italics or underlining
- **B** dash
- **C** colon
- **D** semicolon

**3.** Used in some compound words
- **A** italics or underlining
- **B** colon
- **C** semicolon
- **D** hyphen

**4.** Used to separate hours and minutes in expressions of time
- **A** colon
- **B** semicolon
- **C** dash
- **D** hyphen

**Directions** Mark the choice that correctly completes each sentence.

**5.** The letter began "Dear Mr. ____ I have been a fan of yours for years."
- **A** Benny:
- **B** Benny,
- **C** Benny!
- **D** Benny—

**6.** "I read an article about you in ____ magazine."
- **A** Fanfare
- **B** *Fanfare*
- **C** —Fanfare—
- **D** : Fanfare:

**7.** The band played from ____.
- **A** 715 to 800 p.m.
- **B** 715: to 800: p.m.
- **C** 7:15 to 8:00 p.m.
- **D** 715—800 p.m.

**8.** Kids can sign up for band in sixth ____ wait to join!
- **A** grade? I can't
- **B** grade, I can't
- **C** grade; I can't
- **D** grade-I can't

**9.** Thursday ____ is sign-up day.
- **A** , that's today,
- **B** ; that's today;
- **C** -that's today-
- **D** —that's today—

**10.** The band has ____ members.
- **A** fiftyone
- **B** fifty-one
- **C** fifty:one
- **D** fifty one

**Home Activity** Your child prepared for taking tests on punctuation. Have your child make index cards for the colon, semicolon, dash, hyphen, and italics and then search books and magazines for examples of the use of each mark.

Name ______________________________

# Punctuation

**Directions** Match the punctuation mark with the correct description.

_____ **1.** colon (:) — **A** used to set off material that interrupts

_____ **2.** semicolon (;) — **B** used in some compound words

_____ **3.** dash (—) — **C** used after the salutation of a business letter

_____ **4.** italics (*Big*) — **D** used to join two independent clauses

_____ **5.** hyphen (-) — **E** used to indicate titles

**Directions** Rewrite each sentence. Add the missing punctuation marks.

**6.** Troy doesn't like the old fashioned music that WDQB plays from 1030 to midnight.

______________________________

______________________________

**7.** I began my letter, "Dear Sir Please cancel my subscription to Music Classics."

______________________________

______________________________

**8.** Aunt Kay plays guitar have you heard her? like a pro.

______________________________

______________________________

**9.** One summer vacation I lived with my aunt she was kind to me.

______________________________

______________________________

**10.** She thought I was mature for a ten year old kid she even taught me to play some chords.

______________________________

______________________________

**Home Activity** Your child reviewed punctuation. Have your child make a list of favorite books and magazines with correct underlining.

# Grammar Extra Practice

# Four Kinds of Sentences

**Directions** Write *D* if the sentence is declarative. Write *IN* if the sentence is interrogative. Write *IM* if the sentence is imperative. Write *E* if the sentence is exclamatory.

**1.** I have to write a report on dictionaries. ______

**2.** May I use the encyclopedia to get information? ______

**3.** Use the Internet too. ______

**4.** The library has two computers for public use. ______

**5.** Can the librarian help me get online? ______

**6.** Wow, look at the size of that dictionary! ______

**7.** The introduction gives a great deal of information. ______

**8.** Does it explain what is in the dictionary? ______

**9.** It even has a history of the English language. ______

**10.** I can't believe this dictionary has 225,000 words! ______

**Directions** Complete each sentence with words from the box. Then write *D, IN, IM,* or *E* to identify the kind of sentence.

| | |
|---|---|
| that must have been! | made a fine dictionary in 1758. |
| the first dictionary made? | had to be written by hand. |
| the stacks of paper it took. | |

**11.** How was ______________________________

______

**12.** Samuel Johnson ______________________________

______

**13.** What a lot of work ______________________________

______

**14.** Every definition ______________________________

______

**15.** Imagine ______________________________

______

Name ______________________________



# Subjects and Predicates

**Directions** Draw a line between the complete subject and the complete predicate in each sentence. Circle the simple subject and the simple predicate.

**1.** Many useful tools are made from metal.

**2.** Steel is an important metal for buildings and tools.

**3.** This alloy contains a mixture of iron and carbon.

**4.** An iron bar will rust over time.

**5.** Oxygen from the air mixes with the metal.

**6.** That orange deposit on the outside surface is called rust.

**7.** Many ranchers mend fences regularly.

**Directions** Underline each simple subject once. Underline each simple predicate twice.

**8.** The shiny thin wires are stretched from post to post.

**9.** Someone hammers the wire to the post.

**10.** The wooden posts stretch off in a straight line.

**11.** This job is certainly hard work.

**12.** A work crew will repair the old fence today.

**Directions** Write *F* after a fragment. Write *R* after a run-on. Write *S* after a complete sentence.

**13.** Has been replaced by plastic in many products. ________

**14.** Plastic is hard and durable at the same time, it is lighter than metal. ________

**15.** Many parts of today's trucks and automobiles. ________

**16.** Plastic is not only lighter than metal it is cheaper too. ________

**17.** Just think about all the uses for plastic! ________

**18.** Many new materials from recycled products. ________

Name ______________________

# Independent and Dependent Clauses

**Direction** Write *I* if the underlined group of words is an independent clause. Write *D* if it is a dependent clause.

1. We visited the seashore when we went to California. ______
2. After we walked on the beach, we swam in the ocean. ______
3. Although the sun was warm, I shivered with cold. ______
4. The water seemed even colder because our skin was hot. ______
5. If you look far out, you can see dolphins swimming. ______
6. They leap out of the water as if they are playing. ______
7. While I was resting on the sand, I spied something. ______
8. When I looked through binoculars, I saw they were seals. ______
9. As I watched, some of them slid into the water. ______
10. Since I saw them, I have read more about seals. ______

**Directions** Complete each sentence by adding a clause from the box. Underline the dependent clause in each sentence.

| | | |
|---|---|---|
| it is the exception to the rule | while a seal has none | it can weigh up to 8,800 pounds |
| because walruses are usually much bigger | you will remember it | |

11. You can tell a walrus and a seal apart ______________________
______________________
12. In addition, a walrus has two large ivory tusks ______________________
______________________
13. Because an elephant seal can grow very large, ______________________
______________________
14. If you run into an elephant seal, ______________________
______________________
15. When a male elephant seal is full grown, ______________________
______________________

Name ______________________________



# Compound and Complex Sentences

**Directions** Write *compound* if the sentence is a compound sentence. Write *complex* if the sentence is a complex sentence.

1. Great athletes seem superhuman, but they often begin humbly. ______________
2. After they learned the basics, they practiced hard. ______________
3. If they had failures, they did not give up. ______________
4. They kept at it for years, and they improved. ______________

**Directions** Combine the pairs of simple sentences using the conjunction in ( ). Write the compound sentence on the line.

5. I like swimming. My dad coaches track. (but)

______________________________________________

6. I can jump like a rabbit. I can run like a racehorse. (and)

______________________________________________

7. I could choose one sport. I could do both. (or)

______________________________________________

8. According to Mom, I should decide. She is usually right. (and)

______________________________________________

**Directions** Write the word in ( ) that best connects the clauses. Underline the dependent clause in the complex sentence.

9. The players are tired ______________ they have played two games. (because, if)

10. ______________ they finish their games, they sleep on the bus. (Although, After)

11. They may travel for hours ______________ they reach the next town. (before, since)

12. The driver will not wake them ______________ the bus gets to the hotel. (after, until)

Name ______________________

# Common Nouns and Proper Nouns

**Directions** Write the proper noun from the box that matches each common noun. Add capital letters where they are needed.

| | | |
|---|---|---|
| empire state building | mount everest | aunt lucinda |
| the dark is rising | ms. simpson | |

| Common Noun | Proper Noun |
|---|---|
| **1.** teacher | ______________________ |
| **2.** building | ______________________ |
| **3.** mountain | ______________________ |
| **4.** book | ______________________ |
| **5.** relative | ______________________ |

**Directions** Rewrite each sentence. Capitalize all proper nouns.

**6.** Over sixty years ago aunt rachel was born in russia.

______________________

**7.** She came to the united states during world war II.

______________________

**8.** Her brother is grandpa ozzie.

______________________

**9.** His official title is major oswald schumacher.

______________________

**10.** I write to him at 866 stanley ave., los angeles, ca 90036.

______________________

# Regular and Irregular Plural Nouns

**Directions** Write the plural form of each noun.

**1.** guess ______________

**2.** cocoon ______________

**3.** ax ______________

**4.** branch ______________

**5.** boy ______________

**6.** story ______________

**7.** life ______________

**8.** mouse ______________

**9.** foot ______________

**10.** jacket ______________

**Directions** Underline the plural nouns in each sentence.

**11.** Young children can absorb languages like sponges.

**12.** Their brains attach meanings to sounds at an amazing rate.

**13.** A two-year-old child has twice as many synapses, or connections, in the brain as an adult.

**14.** By the time humans become teenagers, it is much harder for them to learn a foreign language.

**15.** They must learn rules of grammar, translate words from one language to the other, and use learning strategies.

**Directions** Cross out each incorrectly spelled plural noun. Write the correct spelling above the word you crossed out.

**16.** Carly could draw objects such as leafs, berrys, and toys.

**17.** She wanted to draw pictures of animalz, so she took art lessones.

**18.** Now Carly can draw monkeys, mouses, sheeps, deer—any animal you name.

Name ______________________________

# Possessive Nouns

**Directions** Write the possessive form of each underlined noun.

1. mother advice ________________
2. survivor story ________________
3. child toy ________________
4. man overcoat ________________
5. monument history ________________
6. mothers lessons ________________
7. survivors groups ________________
8. children books ________________
9. men clothing ________________
10. monuments construction ________________

**Directions** Rewrite each sentence. Write the possessive form of the underlined noun.

11. A box is tucked away in my grandfather closet.

________________________________________

12. It contains a soldier memories of service.

________________________________________

13. Several pictures edges are worn and crumpled.

________________________________________

14. In those pictures, the young men faces are handsome and smiling.

________________________________________

________________________________________

15. Grandpa treasures his war friends letters and visits.

________________________________________

________________________________________

Name ____________________



# Action and Linking Verbs

**Directions** Underline the verb in each sentence. Write *A* if it is an action verb. Write *L* if it is a linking verb.

**1.** Myths and tales often seem true. ______

**2.** They are important to each civilization. ______

**3.** Myths address basic human questions. ______

**4.** Myths are part of every culture. ______

**5.** Animals often play a role in myths and tales. ______

**6.** These animals speak like people. ______

**7.** Their actions are clever. ______

**8.** Early civilizations understood the value of myths. ______

**9.** They sought answers around them. ______

**10.** Today science, not stories, explains the world. ______

**Directions** Write a verb from the box to complete each sentence. On the line after the sentence, write *A* if the verb is an action verb. Write *L* if it is a linking verb.

| | | | |
|---|---|---|---|
| brought | tells | was | cause |
| seems | honored | frightened | were |

**11.** Early people ____________________ spirits. ______

**12.** Good and evil spirits ____________________ all around them. ______

**13.** Offerings ____________________ the goodwill of spirits. ______

**14.** Scary masks ____________________ away evil spirits. ______

**15.** Sickness ____________________ a sign of evil spirits. ______

**16.** Now this idea ____________________ quaint to us. ______

**17.** Germs, not spirits, ____________________ sickness. ______

**18.** Science ____________________ us this fact. ______

Name ______________________

# Main and Helping Verbs

**Directions** Find the verb phrase in each sentence. Underline the helping verb. Circle the main verb.

1. A new animal shelter has opened in our town.
2. It will provide a temporary home for lost animals.
3. Many pets are abandoned by their owners.
4. The lucky ones are taken to the shelter.
5. They will be fed.
6. They will be treated by a veterinarian.
7. However, these animals should have homes.
8. They have done nothing wrong.
9. Pet owners should take responsibility.
10. Your pets are depending on you.

**Directions** Underline the verb phrase in each sentence. Write *Present* or *Past* to tell the time of the action.

11. American bison have lived in North America for thousands of years. ____________
12. These huge animals are also known as buffalo. ____________
13. Millions of them had long roamed on the Great Plains. ____________
14. In the 1800s, they were hunted mercilessly. ____________
15. Almost all of the buffalo were killed for sport. ____________
16. Cattle ranchers also were invading their grazing land. ____________
17. The last few hundred bison were protected by law in 1905. ____________
18. Today thousands are roaming in parks and refuges. ____________
19. You can see these amazing animals. ____________
20. With people's help, the buffalo has survived. ____________

Name ______________________________

# Subject-Verb Agreement

**Directions** Underline the verb in ( ) that agrees with the subject of each sentence.

1. Today horses (is, are) no longer needed for transportation.
2. We (use, uses) them to ride for pleasure.
3. Some horse lovers (buy, buys) horses of their own.
4. Food and equipment (become, becomes) expensive.
5. Martin (take, takes) riding lessons at a stable.
6. He (enjoy, enjoys) a horse without the responsibilities of ownership.
7. A saddle and bridle (cost, costs) quite a bit.
8. Our family (do, does) not have the land to keep a horse.
9. A dude ranch (offer, offers) accommodations with horse riding privileges.
10. Guests (stay, stays) in a bunkhouse.

**Directions** Add a verb to complete each sentence. Be sure the verb agrees with the subject.

11. Paul Revere's horse ________________ the ground impatiently.
12. Redcoats ________________ the river under cover of night.
13. Two lights ________________ from the church tower.
14. The man and horse ________________ away on their journey.
15. A little moonlight ________________ through the clouds.
16. A warning cry ________________ out in the night.
17. As the sun rises, farmers ________________ their muskets.
18. They ________________ for independence.
19. The fighting ________________ fierce.
20. The colonial militia ________________ the redcoats.

Name ______________________



# Past, Present, and Future Tenses

**Directions** Write the correct present, past, and future tense of each verb.

| Verb | Present | Past | Future |
|---|---|---|---|
| **1.** spy | He ______. | He ______. | He ______. |
| **2.** have | I ______. | I ______. | I ______. |
| **3.** trap | You ______. | You ______. | You ______. |
| **4.** think | She ______. | She ______. | She ______. |
| **5.** eat | They ______. | They ______. | They ______. |

**Directions** Identify the tense of each underlined verb. Write *present, past,* or *future.*

**6.** No one pleases the king these days. ______

**7.** He lost his sense of humor. ______

**8.** We will be happy when he regains it. ______

**9.** The jester tells corny jokes. ______

**10.** He arrived on the scene just in time. ______

**11.** The king laughs heartily. ______

**12.** We will remember this success. ______

**Directions** Rewrite each sentence. Change the underlined verb to the tense in ( ).

**13.** Once, kings rule with complete power. (past)

______________________________

**14.** Now, they serve mainly as figureheads. (present)

______________________________

**15.** Some day perhaps all people govern themselves in democracies. (future)

______________________________

______________________________

Name ______________________

# Principal Parts of Regular Verbs

**Directions** Write *present, present participle, past,* or *past participle* to identity the principal part of the underlined verb.

**1.** What defines genius? ______________

**2.** A genius offers a fresh view. ______________

**3.** Often, the public has rejected ideas of genius at first. ______________

**4.** After time has passed, we understand what was offered. ______________

**5.** People recognized Leonardo's genius at once. ______________

**6.** He concealed many of his ideas in journals. ______________

**7.** Today we are studying them. ______________

**8.** Many of his ideas have appeared as inventions. ______________

**9.** His ideas waited for the right time and place. ______________

**10.** We acknowledge his genius gratefully. ______________

**Directions** Write the sentence using the principal part of the underlined verb indicated in ( ).

**11.** Brilliant ideas change the world. (present participle)

______________________________________________

**12.** Sir Isaac Newton discover universal laws of motion. (past)

______________________________________________

**13.** An object in motion tend to stay in motion. (present)

______________________________________________

**14.** This concept form the basis for the first of his laws of motion. (present)

______________________________________________

**15.** Newton's laws help us understand how the world works. (past participle)

______________________________________________

© Pearson Education

Name ______________________________

# Principal Parts of Irregular Verbs

**Directions** Write *present, present participle, past,* or *past participle* to identify the principal part used to form the underlined verb.

1. Dinosaurs have been extinct for millions of years. ____________
2. The iguanodon was a plant eater. ____________
3. An iguanodon stood about 16 feet tall. ____________
4. It ran on two legs or walked on four. ____________
5. Gideon Mantell had found a few bones in 1822. ____________
6. He had seen the similarity to an iguana. ____________
7. Mantell gave the dinosaur its name. ____________
8. Even today, archaeologists are finding dinosaur bones. ____________
9. Bones and fossils tell us much about extinct animals. ____________
10. We draw conclusions about their size and shape. ____________

**Directions** Write the sentence using the principal part of the underlined verb indicated in ( ).

11. Once all of Earth's land be one big mass. (past)

______________________________________________

12. Over time, it break into pieces. (past)

______________________________________________

13. We now know these pieces moved. (present)

______________________________________________

14. They become the seven continents. (past participle)

______________________________________________

15. Forces inside the Earth make the landmasses move. (past)

______________________________________________

# Troublesome Verbs

**Directions** Write the form of the underlined verb indicated in ( ).

1. Mahalia leave listeners dazzled by her talent. (past) ____________
2. They lay down their troubles for a while. (past) ____________
3. Her success lets other women dream of a career in music. (past) ____________
4. Young Aretha Franklin sit with Mahalia's fans. (past participle) ____________
5. Aretha set goals and achieved them. (past) ____________

**Directions** Underline the verb that correctly completes the sentence.

6. They have (sat, set) in this pew for years.
7. The choir (sat, set) their hymnals on the bench.
8. A bell (lays, lies) on its side.
9. Someone (lay, laid) it there.
10. She has (left, let) a cup of water on the stand.
11. (Leave, Let) us ask for her autograph.
12. The piano (sets, sits) on a platform.

**Directions** Complete each sentence with the correct form of the verb in ( ).

13. Please ____________ with us at the concert. (sit)
14. The singers have ____________ their music down. (set)
15. Yesterday we ____________ our friends at school. (leave)
16. Did you ____________ your guitar at home? (leave)
17. Ms. Guthrie ____________ me pick my recital piece. (let)
18. Yesterday afternoon he ____________ the horn on the table. (lay)
19. The horn has ____________ there ever since. (lay)
20. She will ____________ down and rest before the performance. (lie)

Name ______________________________

# Prepositions and Prepositional Phrases

**Directions** Underline the prepositional phrase in each sentence. Circle the preposition.

**1.** Over the holidays, we had a movie marathon.

**2.** The family watched a series of animated films.

**3.** We have quite a few in our film library.

**4.** I have watched *Dumbo* about 20 times.

**5.** Dumbo is a baby elephant with enormous ears.

**6.** Dumbo stays near his mother.

**7.** She feels protective toward her baby.

**8.** Dumbo finds a great use for his ears.

**9.** Dumbo can fly through the sky.

**10.** He is the biggest hit at the circus.

**Directions** Write *P* if the underlined word is a preposition. Write *O* if it is the object of the preposition.

**11.** Heckle and Jeckle are two crows in *Dumbo*. ________

**12.** They make fun of the baby elephant. ________

**13.** They are amazed when Dumbo soars into the air. ________

**14.** Some encouragement from a little mouse helps Dumbo. ________

**15.** I think the moral is "Believe in yourself." ________

**Directions** Underline the prepositional phrases. The number in ( ) tells how many prepositional phrases are in that sentence.

**16.** The theater is down this street and around a corner. (2)

**17.** Buy four tickets at the booth and two bags of popcorn from the concession stand. (3)

**18.** We always sit toward the back under the balcony. (2)

**19.** At the beginning, it seems very dark in the theater. (2)

**20.** The ads before the show make me hungry for a snack. (2)

Name ______________________



# Subject and Object Pronouns

**Directions** Write *S* if the underlined word is a subject pronoun. Write *O* if the word is an object pronoun.

**1.** In *Weslandia*, Wesley is the main character. He has problems. ______

**2.** Wesley doesn't act like the other kids, and they pick on him. ______

**3.** His parents worry that they have raised an odd son. ______

**4.** Wesley creates a new civilization, and it fascinates everyone. ______

**5.** I really enjoyed reading this story. ______

**6.** Wesley's ingenious uses for his crop amused me. ______

**7.** My friend Winnie said the suntan oil was funniest to her. ______

**8.** You should read this story too! ______

**9.** Our teacher, Mr. Su, asked us about civilizations. ______

**10.** Native peoples create them based on climate and crops in their region. ______

**Directions** Underline the correct pronoun in ( ) to complete each sentence.

**11.** Corn has many uses. Many farmers plant (it, they).

**12.** (They, Them) can sell the grain as a food or as a raw material for fuel.

**13.** The stalks can be ground up. There are several uses for (it, them) as well.

**14.** John and (I, me) have learned about soybeans.

**15.** (We, Us) get nutritious foods from them.

**16.** Do you like tofu? (It, Them) is a curd made from soybeans.

**17.** Mom served tofu to Karl and (I, me).

**18.** She didn't tell (us, we) what we were eating.

**19.** When (he, him) found out it was bean curd, Karl laughed.

**20.** Mom had disguised it in pudding. That was clever of (her, she)!

Name ______________________________

# Pronouns and Antecedents

**Directions** Match the pronoun with the noun or noun phrase that could be its antecedent. Write the letter of the correct antecedent next to the pronoun.

| | | |
|---|---|---|
| _______ | **1.** they | **A** Ellen |
| _______ | **2.** her | **B** James and me |
| _______ | **3.** us | **C** the gym |
| _______ | **4.** he | **D** PE teachers |
| _______ | **5.** it | **E** Dad |

**Directions** Circle the antecedent of the underlined pronoun in each sentence.

**6.** Carl and Dan found out they have the same birthday.

**7.** Angela exercises every day, and she always has energy.

**8.** Jordan swims several miles; he makes it look easy.

**9.** When you exercise them, muscles grow larger and stronger.

**10.** The body must be used to make it work.

**11.** Carmen and I run because we want stronger legs.

**12.** Vary your workouts to keep them interesting.

**Directions** Write a pronoun to replace each underlined noun or noun phrase.

**13.** Our family needs to exercise, so our family joined the YMCA. _______________

**14.** Dad uses the weights because they give Dad the best workout. _______________

**15.** Mom likes swimming, so Mom heads straight for the pool. _______________

**16.** Because Lee and Ava play basketball, Lee and Ava go to the gym. _______________

**17.** When Dad and I have time, Dad and I play tennis together. _______________

**18.** Mom said we should go to the pool with Mom. _______________

**19.** She smiled at Dad and me and told Dad and me that swimming was the best sport. _______________

**20.** Swimming is fine, but swimming is not the best sport; baseball is. _______________

Name ______________________________



# Possessive Pronouns

**Directions** Write the letter of the possessive pronoun that can replace the underlined word or words in each phrase.

_______ **1.** Lori's idea — **A** her

_______ **2.** Nate's paper — **B** their

_______ **3.** the twins' pet — **C** our

_______ **4.** an owl's eyes — **D** its

_______ **5.** Ti's and my cat — **E** his

**Directions** Underline the pronoun that correctly completes each sentence.

**6.** Each ant colony has (its, their) own smell.

**7.** The ants can recognize an intruder in (theirs, their) nest.

**8.** They also know which eggs are not (theirs, we).

**9.** A female worker will help defend (her, she) home.

**10.** I know some ants can sting because an ant stung (mine, my) foot!

**Directions** Write the possessive pronoun that can replace the underlined word or words.

**11.** Dad and I love to have honey on Dad's and my toast. _______

**12.** Mom likes honey on Mom's oatmeal. _______

**13.** Sam puts honey on Sam's peanut butter sandwiches. _______

**14.** Bees make honey for the bees' food. _______

**15.** A bee can always fly back to a bee's hive. _______

**16.** I washed my plate, and now you can wash the plate belonging to you. _______

**17.** Paul put his glass in the dishwasher, and then I added the glass belonging to me. _______

**18.** He found his fork, but she couldn't find the fork belonging to her. _______

Name ______________________________

# Indefinite and Reflexive Pronouns

**Directions** Underline the pronoun in each sentence. Write *indefinite* or *reflexive* to identify the kind of pronoun it is. Then write *singular* or *plural* to show its number.

1. Everybody eats lunch in the cafeteria. ______________ ______________
2. Many of the students bring a sack lunch. ______________ ______________
3. Others eat a hot lunch. ______________ ______________
4. Students help themselves to milk. ______________ ______________
5. Mom says, "Give yourself time to eat." ______________ ______________

**Directions** Underline the correct pronoun in ( ) to complete each sentence.

6. I chose a special place for (myself, myselves).
7. (Everybody, Many) needs a place to be alone and think.
8. (Few, No one) is immune to stress.
9. The teacher said, "Do your work by (theirself, yourself)."
10. (Several, Someone) of my friends have private places.

**Directions** Choose a pronoun from the box to complete each sentence correctly. Be sure indefinite pronouns used as subjects agree in number with their verbs.

| herself | many | myself | something | everybody |
|---|---|---|---|---|

11. If I see someone new, I introduce ______________.
12. I tell the new person ______________ about the school.
13. The new girl said to ______________, "I won't make any friends."
14. ______________ appreciates a friendly welcome.
15. ______________ try to make newcomers feel at home.

Name ______________________________

# Using *Who* and *Whom*

**Directions** Write *subject, object of preposition,* or *direct object* to identify how the underlined word is used.

1. Who likes cheerleading? ______________________
2. Jim is the one for whom the crowd is applauding. ______________________
3. Everyone who is watching was impressed. ______________________
4. Whom will the judges select? ______________________
5. To whom were you speaking? ______________________

**Directions** Underline *who* or *whom* to complete each sentence correctly.

6. (Who, Whom) would like something to drink?
7. Stu is the person to (who, whom) you should give your money.
8. He is the fellow with (who, whom) I went to the concession stand.
9. Anyone (who, whom) watches a gymnastics meet gets thirsty.
10. The judges, (who, whom) are volunteers, do a fantastic job.
11. (Who, Whom) shall we invite next time?
12. It should be someone with (who, whom) you can spend hours.
13. Spectators (who, whom) are veterans bring seat cushions for the bleachers.
14. Everybody (who, whom) sits through the entire gymnastics meet gets sore.
15. For (who, whom) is the meet the most fun?

**Directions** Cross out mistakes in the use of *who* and *whom* in the paragraph. Write the correct pronoun above the line. One sentence is correct.

**(16)** The girl watched her older brother, whom was turning cartwheels. **(17)** He wondered whom else might be looking. **(18)** He fell, and the dog with who the girl had been playing ran to lick his face. **(19)** The girl shrieked with laughter, and the mother, whom had been doing laundry, rushed into the yard. **(20)** "Who is ready for a snack?" asked the mother.

Name ______________________________

# Contractions and Negatives

**Directions** Write the words used to form the contractions.

**1.** wouldn't ____________________

**2.** she'll ____________________

**3.** he's ____________________

**4.** we're ____________________

**5.** isn't ____________________

**6.** can't ____________________

**Directions** Write the contraction for each pair of words.

**7.** will + not ____________

**8.** I + am ____________

**9.** he + had ____________

**10.** you + are ____________

**Directions** Write the contraction for the underlined words.

**11.** What is the worst event you have experienced? ____________

**12.** Grandma said she has lived through tornadoes. ____________

**13.** Bill says he will never forget the earthquake. ____________

**14.** My family is prepared, so we are ready for anything. ____________

**Directions** Circle the word in ( ) that correctly completes each sentence.

**15.** I don't think (any, no) natural disaster is fun to experience.

**16.** Nature doesn't (never, ever) guarantee our safety.

**17.** Often there isn't (nothing, anything) anyone can do.

**18.** We can't (never, ever) be prepared for everything.

Name ______________________________



# Adjectives and Articles

**Directions** Underline the articles and circle the adjectives in each sentence.

**1.** A few brave adventurers are searching for shipwrecks.

**2.** They dive deep beneath the surface in search of an exciting find.

**3.** One group of divers found the treasure of a Spanish galleon.

**4.** The jewels, coins, and other artifacts are priceless.

**5.** Five hundred years ago, these ships sailed from Mexico loaded with silver and gold.

**Directions** Write *what kind, how many,* or *which one* to tell what question each underlined adjective answers about a noun.

**6.** That sunken ship is scary. ______________________

**7.** All tour boats pass by it. ______________________

**8.** The captain explains its tragic wreck. ______________________

**9.** A million tourists have seen it. ______________________

**10.** Some sad songs have been written about it. ______________________

**11.** This song tells about a sailor's wife. ______________________

**12.** She looked for her husband for ten years. ______________________

**Directions** Write *a, an,* or *the* to complete each sentence. Choose the article that makes sense and follows the rules for articles.

**13.** Have you ever found ______________________ real treasure?

**14.** Once I found ______________________ old box.

**15.** It was buried in ______________________ bushes behind my house.

**16.** Inside ______________________ box were some rocks.

**17.** It was ______________________ disappointing moment.

**18.** Later, I found out ______________________ rocks were valuable.

**19.** One rock was ______________________ rare geode.

**20.** It was ______________________ amazing experience.

Name ______________________

# This, That, These, and Those

**Directions** Write *this, that, these,* or *those* to describe each object.

**1.** a book in your hands ______________ book

**2.** a store a mile away ______________ store

**3.** dogs in a neighbor's yard ______________ dogs

**4.** shoes on your feet ______________ shoes

**Directions** Underline the word in ( ) that completes each sentence correctly.

**5.** (That there, That) constellation is called Orion.

**6.** (This, This here) observatory will give us a good view.

**7.** (Them, Those) astronauts who have gone into space have not reached the stars.

**8.** (These, Them) articles tell about their trips to the moon.

**9.** I have reached (this, those) conclusion: Astronauts must be brave.

**10.** Can someone tell me if (this, these) facts are accurate?

**Directions** Write each sentence correctly.

**11.** That there telescope is called the Hubble Telescope.

______________________________________________

______________________________________________

**12.** These here photographs I'm showing you were made by that telescope.

______________________________________________

______________________________________________

**13.** Can you believe that this here photograph shows the birth of a galaxy?

______________________________________________

______________________________________________

**14.** A telescope on Earth could not take them photographs.

______________________________________________

______________________________________________

Name ______________________

# Comparative and Superlative Adjectives

**Directions** Complete the table. Add *-er, -est, more,* or *most* as needed.

| Adjective | Comparative | Superlative |
|---|---|---|
| fierce | **1.** ______ | **6.** ______ |
| small | **2.** ______ | **7.** ______ |
| ridiculous | **3.** ______ | **8.** ______ |
| icy | **4.** ______ | **9.** ______ |
| hot | **5.** ______ | **10.** ______ |

**Directions** Underline the adjective form in ( ) to complete each sentence correctly.

**11.** Which dinosaur was the (stronger, strongest) of all?

**12.** *Triceratops* had a (more dangerous, most dangerous) horn and tail than *Tyrannosaurus*.

**13.** However, *Tyrannosaurus* probably had the (greater, greatest) speed and strength of all the dinosaurs.

**14.** Bill has a (larger, largest) collection of dinosaur figures than I do.

**15.** He has the (more complete, most complete) collection of anyone I know.

**Directions** Write the correct forms of the adjectives in ( ) to complete the sentences.

**16.** Do you think description is ______________ than plot in a story? (important)

**17.** I think stories with good characters are ______________ than stories with good plots. (memorable)

**18.** The ______________ characters of all are the villains. (interesting)

**19.** A ______________ book may not be better than a shorter one. (long)

**20.** The ______________ books of all are the ones that make you think. (good)

Name ______________________________

# Adverbs

**Directions** Write the comparative and superlative forms of each adverb.

| Adverb | Comparative | Superlative |
|---|---|---|
| sadly | 1. ________________ | 5. ________________ |
| wildly | 2. ________________ | 6. ________________ |
| late | 3. ________________ | 7. ________________ |
| well | 4. ________________ | 8. ________________ |

**Directions** Underline the adverb in each sentence. Circle the word or words that each adverb tells more about.

**9.** Settlers waited impatiently for the mail.

**10.** Mail traveled slowly by stagecoach.

**11.** The Pony Express was a very welcome change.

**12.** Riders on horseback raced westward day and night.

**13.** The mail had never moved faster.

**14.** Soon railroads replaced the Pony Express.

**Directions** Underline the correct word in ( ) to complete each sentence.

**15.** The Pony Express moved the mail (most quickly, more quickly) than stagecoaches did.

**16.** The daring riders (certain, certainly) appealed to the public.

**17.** Of all western heroes, these young men lived (more dangerously, most dangerously).

**18.** The Pony Express worked (better, best) for some than for others.

**19.** It cost more to send a letter than most people could (possible, possibly) afford.

**20.** Today, airplanes serve the public (better, best) of all.

Name ______________________________

# Modifiers

**Directions** Underline the adjectives, adverbs, and prepositional phrases in each sentence. (Do not underline the articles *a* and *the*.)

1. Doreen usually swims in the ocean.
2. She thinks the cold water is wonderful.
3. She surfs on the waves and happily collects many shells along the beach.
4. Doreen often swims fifty laps in the pool.
5. The water is warmer, and no salt gets in her eyes.

**Directions** Write *adverb, adjective,* or *prepositional phrase* to identify each underlined modifier. Write *adjective* or *adverb* to identify how a prepositional phrase is used.

6. Several men were fishing on the beach. ____________
7. An artist had set up an easel nearby. ____________
8. Children were digging in the sand. ____________
9. Hungry seagulls drifted above the waves. ____________
10. Sunbathers in swimsuits snoozed in the heat. ____________
11. Some older kids were noisily playing volleyball. ____________
12. A lifeguard in sunglasses sat on a tower. ____________

**Directions** Underline the misplaced modifier in each sentence. Rewrite the sentence, and put the modifier where it belongs.

13. A girl threw a ball to a puppy in a yellow swimsuit.

____________________________________________

____________________________________________

14. I only go to the beach on weekends, never on weekdays.

____________________________________________

____________________________________________

15. A woman signaled to us with a huge dog.

____________________________________________

____________________________________________

Name ______________________________

# Conjunctions

**Directions** Underline the conjunction in each sentence.

**1.** Scientists look for facts and solve problems.

**2.** All problems are different, but each problem takes time to solve.

**3.** Scientists search for answers in an orderly and exact way.

**4.** They use scientific method, or a systematic approach to problem solving.

**5.** Eventually, they form a hypothesis, but this is not the end.

**6.** They must analyze the data and draw a conclusion.

**Directions** Underline the conjunction in ( ) that completes each sentence.

**7.** Is a scientific truth a theory (and, or) a law?

**8.** A theory may be logical, (or, but) a law is widely accepted.

**9.** Newton's ideas about motion are called laws, (and, but) Einstein's idea about relativity is called a theory.

**10.** Both Newton (and, or) Einstein used scientific method.

**Directions** Use the conjunction *and, but,* or *or* to join each pair of sentences. Write the new sentences. Remember to add a comma.

**11.** The reindeer population grew large. Then most of the reindeer died suddenly.

______________________________

______________________________

**12.** Were the reindeer diseased? Did they starve?

______________________________

______________________________

**13.** The animals had lost weight. Their bone marrow contained no fat.

______________________________

______________________________

**14.** The reindeer had eaten all the island's food. Then disaster struck.

______________________________

______________________________

Name ______________________________



# Commas

**Directions** Add commas to each sentence where they are needed.

1. Rafael has joined the Fleet Feet a traveling soccer team.
2. He will have to buy shoes a uniform and a ball.
3. Dad how can I earn money?
4. Well son you could do more chores around the house.
5. Rafael washed the car walked the dog and watered the garden.
6. He also received money as gifts from his aunt grandparents and parents.

**Directions** Rewrite each sentence. Add commas where they are needed.

7. "Anna are you a good money manager?"

_______________________________________________

_______________________________________________

8. In general people are better at spending than saving.

_______________________________________________

_______________________________________________

9. Most people need a budget a plan for keeping track of their income and expenses.

_______________________________________________

_______________________________________________

10. I spend my money on lunches books and supplies.

_______________________________________________

_______________________________________________

11. George a friend who does not have a budget is always short of money.

_______________________________________________

_______________________________________________

12. "By the way George you owe me fifty cents."

_______________________________________________

_______________________________________________

Name ______________________________



# Quotations and Quotation Marks

**Directions** Write *C* if the sentence uses quotation marks and other punctuation correctly. Write *NC* if it is not correct.

**1.** "Are you going to take a vacation," asked Aaron? ______

**2.** "I usually fly to my grandparents' home in Michigan," said Pat. ______

**3.** "Do you like to fly," asked Aaron, "or would you rather take a train?" ______

**4.** "Pat replied, I like different things about both." ______

**5.** "A train lets you see more things," she explained. "However, an airplane is quicker." ______

**Directions** Write each sentence correctly. Add capital letters, quotation marks, and other punctuation as needed.

**6.** when does our flight take off asked Nina

______________________________

**7.** it is scheduled to leave at 8:00 A.M. said Mom

______________________________

**8.** she added that means we should be at the airport by 6:00 A.M.

______________________________

______________________________

**9.** no way cried Nina that's too early

______________________________

**10.** it is early agreed Mom however, we have to allow plenty of time

______________________________

______________________________

**11.** after we check our bags she suggested we can have breakfast

______________________________

______________________________

**12.** that sounds good said Nina can I buy a magazine to read

______________________________

______________________________

Name ______________________

# Punctuation

**Directions** Match the punctuation with a description of its use.

| | | | |
|---|---|---|---|
| ______ | **1.** italics (underlining) | **A** | join clauses without a conjunction |
| ______ | **2.** colons (:) | **B** | express hours and minutes and appear after salutation in business letter |
| ______ | **3.** dashes (—) | **C** | join some compound words |
| ______ | **4.** semicolons (;) | **D** | set off titles of books, magazines, and works of art |
| ______ | **5.** hyphens (-) | **E** | set off words that interrupt the sentence |

**Directions** Rewrite each sentence. Add the missing punctuation marks.

**6.** I'm always losing things I can usually find them in a few minutes.

______________________________

______________________________

**7.** I have lost six notebooks, twenty one pencils, and my America Sings book.

______________________________

______________________________

**8.** Now my jacket it's the one with the gold buttons is missing.

______________________________

______________________________

**9.** It could be in the car it might be in my locker.

______________________________

______________________________

**10.** There's one thing this ten year old will never forget. School ends at 345 P.M.!

______________________________

______________________________

# Standardized Test Preparation

Name ______________________________

# Language Test

Read the passage and decide which type of mistake, if any, appears in each underlined section. Mark the letter of your answer.

*The Swiss Family Robinson,* by Johann david Wyss (1), is an adventure story for all ages. When these six people are shipwrecked on a tropical island they (2) must meet the challenge to survive. In fact, they succeed in creating a new life for themselfs. (3) The family's active (4) imagination helps it figure out ways to farm, build, and tame wild animals. Would love to live in their (5) treehouse. Action and adventures waits (6) on every page.

1. **A** Spelling
   **B** Capitalization
   **C** Punctuation
   **D** No mistake

2. **F** Spelling
   **G** Capitalization
   **H** Punctuation
   **J** No mistake

3. **A** Spelling
   **B** Capitalization
   **C** Punctuation
   **D** No mistake

4. **F** Spelling
   **G** Capitalization
   **H** Punctuation
   **J** No mistake

5. **A** Missing sentence part
   **B** Verb tense
   **C** Subject-verb agreement
   **D** No mistake

6. **F** Missing sentence part
   **G** Verb tense
   **H** Subject-verb agreement
   **J** No mistake

Name ______________________________

# Writing Test

Read the paragraph and answer questions 1–4.

(1) Tie a string around an apple, as though cutting it in half from top to bottom. (2) Then wrap the string around the apple at right angles to the first string and tie it at the top. (3) Do you know how to make a square knot? (4) Next, spread peanut butter over the outside of the apple. (5) Now roll the delicious fruit in a bowl that you previously filled with birdseed until you can no longer see peanut butter through the birdseed. (6) Hang your feeder by its string to a nail hammered into a tree trunk.

**1.** Which sentence should be left out of this paragraph?

**A** Sentence 1
**B** Sentence 3
**C** Sentence 4
**D** Sentence 6

**2.** Which sentence is the best revision of sentence 5?

**F** Now roll it in birdseed until you can no longer see the peanut butter through the birdseed.
**G** Now roll the apple in a bowl of birdseed until it is covered.
**H** Cover the apple with birdseed.
**J** Take the apple and put it in birdseed and cover it with birdseed.

**3.** Which transition would be a good addition to sentence 6?

**A** Before going farther,
**B** However,
**C** Finally,
**D** As a third step,

**4.** Which sentence has the best voice and mood to end this paragraph?

**F** We must do our best to assist our dear feathered friends.
**G** Your difficult task has come to an end.
**H** I hope you enjoy watching the birds as much as I do.
**J** The birds will polish off every bit of this feeder, except the string!

Name ______________________

# Language Test

Read the passage and decide which type of mistake, if any, appears in each underlined section. Mark the letter of your answer.

Many people consider Thomas Alva Edison to be the greatest inventer of all time (1). Not only did he perfect the light bulb, but he also sit up the first (2) electrical power company. What is more, he invents the phonograph and (3) improved the telegraph, the telephone, and motion picture technology. He established a research laboratory and produced most of him inventions (4) from that laboratory. Amazingly, Edison obtained 1,093 United States patents—about one every two weeks of his working life (5). This record surprised even Edison hisself (6).

1. A Spelling
   B Capitalization
   C Punctuation
   D No mistake

2. F Prepositional phrase error
   G Pronoun-antecedent error
   H Verb error
   J No mistake

3. A Prepositional phrase error
   B Verb error
   C Pronoun-antecedent error
   D No mistake

4. F Prepositional phrase error
   G Verb error
   H Possessive pronoun error
   J No mistake

5. A Prepositional phrase error
   B Pronoun-antecedent error
   C Possessive pronoun error
   D No mistake

6. F Subject-verb agreement error
   G Reflexive pronoun error
   H Possessive pronoun error
   J No mistake

Name ______________________________

# Writing Test

Read the paragraph and answer questions 1–4.

(1) *Dinosaur* means "terrible lizard," but how do dinosaurs compare to today's lizards? (2) The body covering of both animals is similar—a tough, dry skin covered in scales. (3) Nonetheless, while the dinosaur was a sort of first cousin to the ancient reptiles, dinosaurs differed in several ways. (4) Dinosaurs had powerful legs that moved directly under the body, but reptiles' legs extend out to the sides. (5) Think about how a lizard moves, slowly, with side-to-side motion; compare this to the strong-legged, swift *Tyrannosaurus rex*. (6) Some scientists think that dinosaurs were related to birds. (7) In addition, dinosaurs had skulls designed for strength, for grasping and tearing prey.

**1.** Which sentence does not stick to the topic?

**A** Sentence 1
**B** Sentence 3
**C** Sentence 4
**D** Sentence 6

**2.** Which sentence is the best choice for topic sentence?

**F** Sentence 7
**G** Sentence 4
**H** Sentence 2
**J** Sentence 1

**3.** Which sentence elaborates on the idea of differences between dinosaurs and lizards?

**A** Sentence 2
**B** Sentence 3
**C** Sentence 5
**D** Sentence 6

**4.** Which of the following sentences would be a good conclusion for this paragraph?

**F** Strong, swift dinosaurs were better suited to prehistoric life than lizards, their modern cousins.
**G** Dinosaurs and lizards were as different as night and day.
**H** Both lizards and dinosaurs seem creepy and scary to me.
**J** It seems odd that scientists think dinosaurs are similar to birds, since they had no feathers.

Name ____________________

# Language Test

Read the passage and decide which type of mistake, if any, appears in each underlined section. Mark the letter of your answer.

It took ten years and six tries, but Steve Fossett wouldnt give up. (1) On July 2, 2002, he became the first person around the world (2) to pilot a balloon solo. This remarkable feat took 13 days, 8 hours, 33 minutes and it involved (3) moving in the jet stream at speeds up to 200 miles per hour. Imagine doing this task all alone and being able to sleep only (4) for short periods. In all his attempts to circumnavigate, or travel around the world, Fossett faced the most terrifyingest storms (5) and other problems. Describing his feelings about his success, Fossett said, It's enormous (6) relief and satisfaction."

1. A Spelling
   B Capitalization
   C Punctuation
   D No mistake

2. F Double negative
   G Misplaced modifier
   H Conjunction error
   J No mistake

3. A Conjunction error
   B Misplaced modifier
   C Comma error
   D No mistake

4. F Comma error
   G Conjunction error
   H Misplaced modifier
   J No mistake

5. A Quotation error
   B Comparative adjective error
   C Conjunction error
   D No mistake

6. F Quotation error
   G Comma error
   H Conjunction error
   J No mistake

Name ______________________________

# Writing Test

Read the paragraph and answer questions 1–4.

(1) The 1883 eruption of the volcano on Krakatoa affected the world profoundly. (2) It released four times the energy of the biggest human-made bomb. (3) Scientists think that Krakatoa had another major eruption in A.D. 416 (4) The 1883 explosions were heard over a third of the Earth's surface. (5) Shock waves from the explosions circled the Earth seven times, and darkness fell on the area. (6) The most lasting effects resulted from volcanic ash. (7) It encircled the globe. (8) For years, Earth's temperatures were lowered as much as 1.2° Centigrade, and people observed spectacular red sunsets and blue and green suns.

**1.** Which sentence is the paragraph's topic sentence?

**A** Sentence 1
**B** Sentence 3
**C** Sentence 4
**D** Sentence 6

**2.** Which is the best way to combine sentences 6 and 7?

**F** The most lasting effects encircled the globe.
**G** The most lasting effects resulted from the volcanic ash but encircled the globe.
**H** The most lasting effects resulted from the volcanic ash who encircled the globe.
**J** The most lasting effects resulted from volcanic ash that encircled the globe.

**3.** Which of the following sentences is the best paraphrase of sentences 6, 7, and 8?

**A** Volcanoes can lower Earth's temperature and change climates.
**B** Krakatoa's volcanic ash lowered temperatures and colored the view of the sun worldwide.
**C** Volcanic ash from the Krakatoa explosion drifted around the world.
**D** The colors we see can be changed by adding dust to Earth's atmosphere.

**4.** Which sentence could be deleted?

**F** Sentence 2
**G** Sentence 3
**H** Sentence 5
**J** Sentence 7

# Unit Writing Lessons

Name ________________________________________

# Notes for a Personal Narrative

**Directions** Fill in the graphic organizer with information about the event or experience that you plan to write about.

## Summary

**What happened?** ________________________________________

**When?** ________________________________________

**Where?** ________________________________________

**Who was there?** ________________________________________

## Details

**Beginning**

**Middle**

**End**

© Pearson Education

Name ______________________________

# Words That Tell About *You*

**Directions** How did you feel about the challenge facing you at the beginning, middle, and end of your experience? Choose one or two words from the word bank to describe each part of your experience. Then add details that *show* readers each feeling.

| anxious | thrilled | proud | inspired |
|---|---|---|---|
| disappointed | excited | contented | determined |
| dismayed | fearful | delighted | upset |

**Beginning** ______________________________

______________________________

______________________________

______________________________

______________________________

**Middle** ______________________________

______________________________

______________________________

______________________________

______________________________

**End** ______________________________

______________________________

______________________________

______________________________

______________________________

© Pearson Education

Name ______________________________

# Elaboration

## Combine Sentences

When you write, you can elaborate by combining short simple sentences to make compound or complex sentences. This will create a smoother flow of ideas in your writing. The two sentences you combine must make sense together. You can create compound sentences by combining short sentences using the words *and, but,* or *or.* You can create complex sentences by combining short sentences with *if, because, before, after, since,* or *when.*

**Directions** Use the word in ( ) to combine the two sentences. Remember to capitalize the first word of the new sentence and to replace the first period with a comma.

**1.** (but) My big sister could climb the pine tree in the pasture. I had not tried.

______________________________

______________________________

**2.** (because) The first limbs were so high. I thought it was too hard.

______________________________

______________________________

**3.** (when) She boosted me up. I could just reach the lowest limb.

______________________________

______________________________

**4.** (and) The rough bark scratched my skin. Sticky pine resin oozed onto my hands.

______________________________

______________________________

**5.** (but) I was scared. I climbed to the very top of that pine.

______________________________

______________________________

© Pearson Education

Name ______________________________

# Self-Evaluation Guide

## Personal Narrative

**Directions** Think about the final draft of your personal narrative. Then rate yourself on a scale from 4 to 1 (4 is the highest) on each writing trait. After you fill out the chart, answer the questions.

| Writing Traits | 4 | 3 | 2 | 1 |
|---|---|---|---|---|
| Focus/Ideas | | | | |
| Organization/Paragraphs | | | | |
| Voice | | | | |
| Word Choice | | | | |
| Sentences | | | | |
| Conventions | | | | |

**1.** What is the best part of your personal narrative? Why?

______________________________

______________________________

______________________________

______________________________

**2.** Write one thing you would change about this personal narrative if you had the chance to write it again. Why?

______________________________

______________________________

______________________________

______________________________

© Pearson Education

Name ______________________________

# How-to Chart

**Directions** Fill in the graphic organizer with information about your project.

**Explain Task** ______________________________

______________________________

______________________________

**Materials** ______________________________

______________________________

______________________________

**Introduction** ______________________________

______________________________

______________________________

______________________________

**Steps** ______________________________

______________________________

______________________________

______________________________

______________________________

______________________________

______________________________

**Conclusion** ______________________________

______________________________

______________________________

© Pearson Education

Name ______________________________

# Time-Order Words

**Directions** Add a time-order word to each of the five steps below. Write each sentence. Then add a final sentence using a time-order word. Tell what would happen in the last step.

1. Grab a soccer ball and head to the field.

______________________________

______________________________

2. Stand about five feet in front of the goal posts.

______________________________

______________________________

3. Take five steps back and two large steps to the left.

______________________________

______________________________

4. Drop the ball to the ground in front of you.

______________________________

______________________________

5. Wind up and kick that soccer ball as hard as you can toward the goal.

______________________________

______________________________

6. ______________________________

______________________________

Name ______________________________

# Elaboration

## Strong Action Verbs

When you write, you can elaborate by using strong action verbs. The right action verbs make your writing more vivid and interesting to readers.

**Vague** Last night, snow fell in our city.
**Specific** Last night, snow blanketed our city.

**Directions** Replace each underlined word with an action verb. Write each sentence.

**1.** After a heavy snowfall, I love to make a snowman.

______________________________

______________________________

**2.** Begin by getting the largest snowball you can.

______________________________

______________________________

**3.** Then move the snowball through the snow.

______________________________

______________________________

**4.** Next, put three of these giant snowballs one on top of the other.

______________________________

______________________________

**5.** Finally, put your snowman in clothes, a scarf, or a hat.

______________________________

______________________________

Name ______________________________

# Self-Evaluation Guide

## How-to Report

**Directions** Think about the final draft of your how-to report. Then rate yourself on a scale from 4 to 1 (4 is the highest) on each writing trait. After you fill out the chart, answer the questions.

| Writing Traits | 4 | 3 | 2 | 1 |
|---|---|---|---|---|
| Focus/Ideas | | | | |
| Organization/Paragraphs | | | | |
| Voice | | | | |
| Word Choice | | | | |
| Sentences | | | | |
| Conventions | | | | |

**1.** What is the best part of your how-to report?

______________________________

______________________________

______________________________

______________________________

______________________________

**2.** Write one thing you would change about this how-to report if you had the chance to write it again.

______________________________

______________________________

______________________________

______________________________

______________________________

© Pearson Education

Name ______________________________

# Venn Diagram

**Directions** Fill in the Venn diagram with similarities and differences about the two things you are comparing.

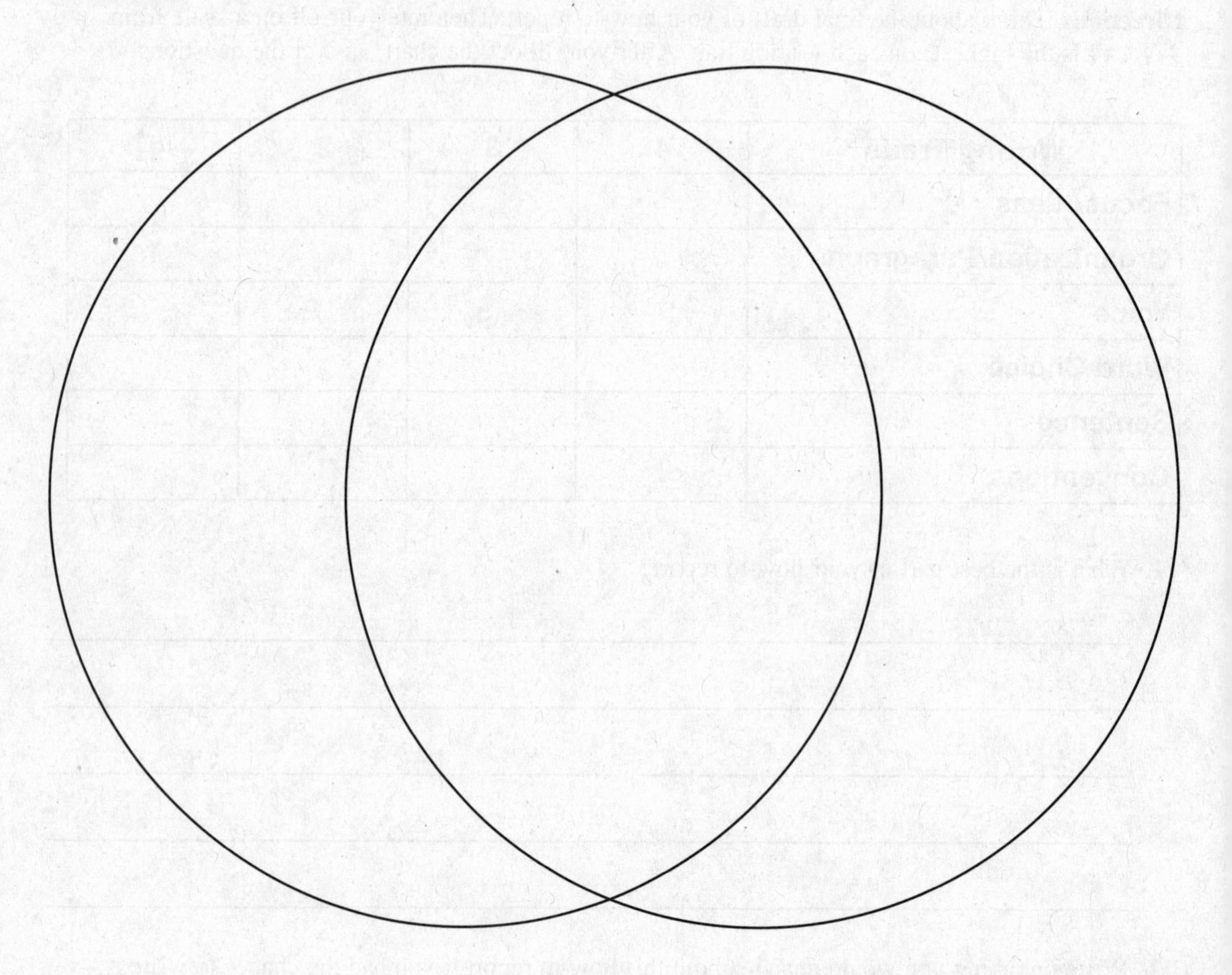

© Pearson Education

Name ______________________________

# Words That Compare and Contrast

**Directions** The words in the box signal that two things are alike or different. Write two sentences that explain how your two inventions are alike, using words from the box. Then write two sentences that explain how your two inventions are different, using words from the box.

| Words That Signal Similarity | Words That Signal Difference |
|---|---|
| and | but |
| also | however |
| too | unlike |
| as well | on the other hand |
| like | |

**How the two things are alike**

**1.** ______________________________

______________________________

______________________________

**2.** ______________________________

______________________________

______________________________

**How the two things are different**

**1.** ______________________________

______________________________

______________________________

**2.** ______________________________

______________________________

______________________________

Name ______________________________

# Elaboration

## Parallelism

If a sentence has parts that are alike, those parts should have the same form or pattern. **Parallelism,** or **parallel structure,** refers to the pattern, or organization, of similar sentence parts, such as verbs or adjectives.

| | |
|---|---|
| **Not Parallel** | Riders were expected to ride a horse, facing dangers, and go for hours without sleep. |
| **Parallel** | Riders were expected to ride a horse, face dangers, and go for hours without sleep. |

**Directions** Rewrite the sentences to make them parallel.

**1.** The Pony Express carried mail, rode long distances, and they travel at 10 miles per hour.

______________________________

______________________________

**2.** Today, e-mail makes modern communication much quicker, cheaper, and easy to use.

______________________________

______________________________

**3.** Riders for the Pony Express rode 75–100 miles at a time, changed horses every 10–15 miles, and are earning $100 a month.

______________________________

______________________________

**4.** Unlike the Pony Express, you can send an e-mail, are receiving a reply, and respond in just minutes!

______________________________

______________________________

**5.** Do you communicate by e-mail, letters, or talking on the telephone?

______________________________

Name ______________________________

# Self-Evaluation Guide

## Compare and Contrast Essay

**Directions** Think about the final draft of your compare and contrast essay. Then rate yourself on a scale from 4 to 1 (4 is the highest) on each writing trait. After you fill out the chart, answer the questions.

| Writing Traits | 4 | 3 | 2 | 1 |
|---|---|---|---|---|
| Focus/Ideas | | | | |
| Organization/Paragraphs | | | | |
| Voice | | | | |
| Word Choice | | | | |
| Sentences | | | | |
| Conventions | | | | |

1. What is the best part of your compare and contrast essay?

______________________________

______________________________

______________________________

______________________________

2. Write one thing you would change about this compare and contrast essay if you had the chance to write it again.

______________________________

______________________________

______________________________

______________________________

© Pearson Education

Name ______________________________

# Story Chart

**Directions** Fill in the story chart with the characters, setting, events, and solution for your story.

## Title

## Characters

## Setting

## Events

## Solution

© Pearson Education

Name ______________________________

# Good Beginnings

**Directions** Practice writing sentences that will grab your reader's attention. Using your story idea as the topic, write one sentence for each strategy. You can use one of the sentences to start your first draft.

**1.** Ask a question.

______________________________

______________________________

**2.** Use an exclamation.

______________________________

______________________________

**3.** Use a sound word.

______________________________

______________________________

**4.** Hint at the ending.

______________________________

______________________________

**5.** Use a simile.

______________________________

______________________________

**6.** Make a list.

______________________________

______________________________

**7.** Set the scene.

______________________________

______________________________

Name ______________________________

# Elaboration

## Pronouns

**Directions** The sentences below need a pronoun or an antecedent. Replace the underlined word or words with an appropriate pronoun or antecedent.

1. It is so useful. Did you ever wonder who invented it?

______________________________

______________________________

2. I've had my skateboard for so long, my skateboard is covered in stickers.

______________________________

______________________________

3. Beth is such a great singer because Beth has been taking lessons since Beth was five years old.

______________________________

______________________________

4. She is the best runner in class. No one can beat her in the 50-yard dash.

______________________________

______________________________

5. Dan left for school without it, and he had to call home and ask his mom to bring it to him.

______________________________

______________________________

6. John asked if John could go to the movies Friday night.

______________________________

______________________________

Name ________________________________

# Self-Evaluation Guide

## Story

**Directions** Think about the final draft of your story. Then rate yourself on a scale from 4 to 1 (4 is the highest) on each writing trait. After you fill out the chart, answer the questions.

| Writing Traits | 4 | 3 | 2 | 1 |
|---|---|---|---|---|
| Focus/Ideas | | | | |
| Organization/Paragraphs | | | | |
| Voice | | | | |
| Word Choice | | | | |
| Sentences | | | | |
| Conventions | | | | |

**1.** What is the best part of your story?

______________________________________________

______________________________________________

______________________________________________

______________________________________________

______________________________________________

**2.** Write one thing you would change about this story if you had the chance to write it again.

______________________________________________

______________________________________________

______________________________________________

______________________________________________

______________________________________________

Name ______________________________

# Persuasive Argument Chart

**Directions** Fill in the graphic organizer with ideas for the introduction, supporting reasons, and conclusion in your persuasive essay.

**Introduction: State your opinion or goals**

↓

**First reason**

↓

**Second reason**

↓

**Third reason (most important)**

↓

**Conclusion**

Name ______________________________

# Persuasive Words

**Directions** Add a persuasive word from the box or a word of your own to each sentence. Rewrite the sentence.

**Persuasive Words**

| | | | | |
|---|---|---|---|---|
| better | worse | should | never | most important |
| best | worst | must | necessary | effective |

**1.** A camping trip in the Alaskan wilderness is the _____ excursion for our class.

______________________________

______________________________

**2.** It is _____ to set up camp away from any bear habitats.

______________________________

______________________________

**3.** Plenty of protective gear is _____ for survival.

______________________________

______________________________

**4.** While camping in Alaska, we'll learn that teamwork is _____ than working alone in the wilderness.

______________________________

______________________________

**5.** You _____ experience the wide-open spaces on our adventure in Alaska.

______________________________

______________________________

Name ______________________________

# Elaboration

## Descriptive Words

**Directions** Rewrite each sentence using the correct form of the adjective in parentheses.

**1.** What could be (good) than exploring a deserted island in the Pacific?

______________________________

______________________________

______________________________

**2.** Traveling by plane is the (memorable) way to get to the island because you land on the beach!

______________________________

______________________________

______________________________

**3.** Going by boat is (popular) than flying, but it is much slower, and some students may get seasick.

______________________________

______________________________

______________________________

**4.** There are many activities we can do on the island, some (easy) and others (challenging).

______________________________

______________________________

______________________________

**5.** I chose the (spectacular) destination I could think of because I want this trip to be the adventure of a lifetime!

______________________________

______________________________

______________________________

Name ______________________

# Self-Evaluation Guide

## Persuasive Essay

**Directions** Think about the final draft of your persuasive essay. Then rate yourself on a scale from 4 to 1 (4 is the highest) on each writing trait. After you fill out the chart, answer the questions.

| Writing Traits | 4 | 3 | 2 | 1 |
|---|---|---|---|---|
| Focus/Ideas | | | | |
| Organization/Paragraphs | | | | |
| Voice | | | | |
| Word Choice | | | | |
| Sentences | | | | |
| Conventions | | | | |

**1.** What is the best part of your persuasive essay?

______________________

______________________

______________________

______________________

______________________

**2.** Write one thing you would change about this persuasive essay if you had the chance to write it again.

______________________

______________________

______________________

______________________

______________________

Name ______________________________

# K-W-L Chart

**Directions** Fill out this K-W-L chart to help you organize your ideas.

**Topic** ______________________________

| What I Know | What I Want to Know | What I Learned |
|---|---|---|
| | | |

**Controlling Question** ______________________________

Name ______________________________

# Topic and Detail Sentences

**Directions** Decide how you will organize your paragraphs. Then write a topic sentence and supporting details for each paragraph.

**Paragraph 1**
Topic Sentence ______________________________

______________________________

Detail Sentences ______________________________

______________________________

______________________________

**Paragraph 2**
Topic Sentence ______________________________

______________________________

Detail Sentences ______________________________

______________________________

______________________________

**Paragraph 3**
Topic Sentence ______________________________

______________________________

Detail Sentences ______________________________

______________________________

______________________________

**Paragraph 4**
Topic Sentence ______________________________

______________________________

Detail Sentences ______________________________

______________________________

______________________________

© Pearson Education

Name ______________________________

# Elaboration

## Combine Sentences

**Directions** Use the word in parentheses to combine each pair of sentences. Remember to capitalize the first word of each new sentence and to add a comma when necessary.

**1.** (because) You can't see faults. They are far below the surface of the Earth.

______________________________

______________________________

**2.** (when) An earthquake occurs. Parts of the Earth's crust suddenly break and shift.

______________________________

______________________________

______________________________

**3.** (or) Are all earthquake waves the same? Are there different kinds of earthquake waves?

______________________________

______________________________

______________________________

**4.** (and) The Richter scale measures energy released. The Mercali scale measures the results of an earthquake.

______________________________

______________________________

______________________________

**5.** (but) Today geologists can neither predict nor prevent earthquakes. One day they hope to do both.

______________________________

______________________________

______________________________

© Pearson Education

Name ____________________________________________

# Self-Evaluation Guide

## Research Report

**Directions** Think about the final draft of your research report. Then rate yourself on a scale from 4 to 1 (4 is the highest) on each writing trait. After you fill out the chart, answer the questions.

| Writing Traits | 4 | 3 | 2 | 1 |
|---|---|---|---|---|
| Focus/Ideas | | | | |
| Organization/Paragraphs | | | | |
| Voice | | | | |
| Word Choice | | | | |
| Sentences | | | | |
| Conventions | | | | |

**1.** What is the best part of your research report?

________________________________________________

________________________________________________

________________________________________________

________________________________________________

________________________________________________

**2.** Write one thing you would change about this research report if you had the chance to write it again.

________________________________________________

________________________________________________

________________________________________________

________________________________________________

________________________________________________